MoRe
TooLs
for Teaching
Social Skills in
ScHOOL

Grades 3–12

RAUL H. CASTRO MIDDLE SCHOOL
2730 N. 79TH AVENUE
PHOENIX, ARIZONA 85035

Also from the Boys Town Press

The Well-Managed Classroom, 2nd Edition
Tools for Teaching Social Skills in School
Show Me Your Mad Face
Great Days Ahead: Parenting Children Who Have ADHD with Hope and Confidence
Safe and Healthy Secondary Schools
Teaching Social Skills to Youth, 2nd Edition
Effective Study Strategies for Every Classroom
Tips and Tools for Implementing a Classroom Management System DVD
Working with Aggressive Youth
No Room for Bullies
No Room for Bullies: Lesson Plans for Grades 5-8
Competing with Character®
The 100-Yard Classroom
Changing Children's Behavior by Changing the People, Places, and Activities in Their Lives
Adolescence and Other Temporary Mental Disorders DVD
Raising Children without Losing Your Voice or Your Mind DVD
Common Sense Parenting® DVDs:
> Building Relationships
> Teaching Children Self-Control
> Correcting Misbehavior
> Preventing Problem Behavior
> Teaching Kids to Make Good Decisions
> Helping Kids Succeed in School

Common Sense Parenting®
Common Sense Parenting® of Toddlers and Preschoolers
Common Sense Parenting® Learn-at-Home DVD Kit
Time to Enrich Before and After School Activity Kit
Dealing with Your Kids' 7 Biggest Troubles
Good Night, Sweet Dreams, I Love You: Now Get into Bed and Go to Sleep
Parenting to Build Character in Your Teen
Practical Tools for Foster Parents
Skills for Families, Skills for Life, 2nd Edition

For Adolescents
Friend Me!
Guys, Let's Keep It Real
Little Sisters, Listen Up
Boundaries: A Guide for Teens
A Good Friend
Who's in the Mirror?
What's Right for Me?

For Children
The WORST Day of My Life EVER!
I Just Don't Like the Sound of NO!
SORRY, I Forgot to Ask!
Making Friends Is an Art!
Teamwork Isn't My Thing and I Don't
> Like to Share
Cliques Just Don't Make Cents
Getting Along with Others

For a Boys Town Press catalog, call **1-800-282-6657**
or visit our website: **BoysTownPress.org**

Boys Town National Hotline®
1-800-448-3000
A crisis, resource and referral number for kids and parents

MoRe ToOLs for Teaching Social Skills in ScHOOL

Grades 3–12

35 Lesson Plans with Activities, Role-Plays, Worksheets, and Skill Posters to Improve Student Behavior

Midge Odermann Mougey, Ed.D., Jo C. Dillon, Denise Pratt

BOYS TOWN Press®

Boys Town, Nebraska

More Tools for Teaching Social Skills in School
Published by the Boys Town Press
14100 Crawford St.
Boys Town, NE 68010

Copyright © 2009, Father Flanagan's Boys' Home
ISBN: 978-1-934490-04-4

The Boys Town Press is the publishing division
of Boys Town, a national organization serving
children and families.

Publisher's Cataloging in Publication

Mougey, Midge Odermann.

More tools for teaching social skills in school /
Midge Odermann Mougey, Ed. D., Jo C. Dillon and
Denise Pratt. -- 1st ed. -- Boys Town, Neb. : Boys
Town Press, 2009.

p. ; cm. + 1 CD-ROM (4 3/4 in.)

ISBN: 978-1-934490-04-4
Accompanied by a CD-ROM which includes
reproducible worksheets and skill posters.

1. Social skills--Study and teaching. 2. Social
skills in children. 3. Classroom management.
4. Interpersonal relations in children. 5. Child
psychology. I. Dillon, Jo C. II. Pratt, Denise.
III. Title.

10 9 8 7 6 5 4 3

Acknowledgments

This workbook is a testament to the effort and dedication of countless colleagues who helped research, develop, refine and implement the Boys Town educational philosophy and its teaching methods. We applaud their work to improve the lives of America's children. We also want to say a special "Thank you" to Boys Town staffers Michele Hensley and Kathleen McGee for providing creative ideas and activities that enhanced these lesson plans, and to Susan Lamke for her guidance and support.

Table of Contents

Introduction

Lesson Plans

Lesson Plans for Social Skills Instruction

Why won't Frankie ever follow my instructions?

If Lilly would just listen the FIRST time I explain the assignments, we wouldn't waste so much time.

Can Connor ever stop complaining?

If that child went a week without forgetting something, I'd go speechless from shock.

You may never have uttered thoughts like these in the classroom, but you've surely said (maybe even screamed) them in your head. Student behavior, from the mildly irritating to the absolutely infuriating, can drive even the most committed teacher to distraction.

Today's classrooms are filled with students who have divergent life experiences, histories and families. As a result, the social skills and social abilities they display are neither universal nor uniform. If you expect or assume that students should know how to follow instructions, stay on task, work cooperatively, communicate honestly or manage their emotions, you shouldn't. Many will walk into your classroom lacking the skills necessary to be consistently successful in school. Some may possess a range of social skills but struggle to adapt or transfer them to the classroom. Others simply have had no formal instruction or guidance. They rely on their own habits and devices to get their needs met. Unfortunately, these habits do not always conform to the standards of acceptable behavior. And the more time you

have to spend correcting misbehaviors, the less time you have to teach academics.

The lesson plans in *More Tools for Teaching Social Skills in School* are designed to help you empower every student to be more successful, regardless of circumstance or environment. Through social skills instruction, you can give students more behavioral choices, choices that are healthier and more productive for them and for you. Teaching young people new ways of thinking, new ways of feeling good and new ways of behaving can have a transformative effect in your classroom. Research shows that social skills instruction, in addition to other classroom management practices, can decrease aggressive behavior and increase academic engagement. When students learn to use the skills outlined in this workbook, they can help you create the productive, collaborative and cooperative learning environment that you desire and they deserve.

How to Use This Workbook

Each of the thirty-five lesson plans focuses on a specific social skill, broken down into its behavioral steps: Greeting Others, Setting Goals, Being Prepared for Class, Following Instructions, Staying on Task, Getting the Teacher's Attention, Contributing to Discussions (Joining in a Conversation), Listening to Others, Completing Homework, Making a Request (Asking a Favor), Accepting "No" for an Answer, Accepting Criticism or a Consequence, Disagreeing Appropriately,

Advocating for Oneself, Making an Appropriate Complaint, Choosing Appropriate Words to Say, Accepting Decisions of Authority, Using Anger-Control Strategies, Making an Apology (Saying You're Sorry), Expressing Empathy and Understanding for Others, Giving Compliments, Showing Appreciation, Accepting Awards and Honors, Accepting Compliments, Going to an Assembly, Accepting Winning Appropriately, Accepting Defeat or Loss, Choosing Appropriate Friends, Setting Appropriate Boundaries, Extending an Offer or Invitation, Declining an Offer or Invitation Graciously, Resisting Negative Peer Pressure, Responding to/Reporting Inappropriate Talk or Touch, Reporting Other Youths' Behavior (Peer Reporting) and Communicating Honestly.

We have included many of the sixteen skills that are the foundation of Boys Town's Well-Managed Classroom, and these lesson plans give you different teaching activities than those found in the original *Tools for Teaching Social Skills in School* book. You also will find more than a dozen new skills, from the basic to the complex. Some lessons cover "simple" social skills that may be of particular interest to elementary educators. However, if you teach

in junior or senior high school, you can still use these lessons as reviews for students and to reinforce your behavioral expectations. Other lessons focus on more advanced skills. Because so many student misbehaviors and classroom meltdowns result from unhealthy relationships, especially with teens, there are lessons to help you address problems related to inappropriate language and unhealthy boundaries.

All of the lessons follow the same general outline, beginning with "Teacher Notes." The notes include background information about a skill and its relevance to the classroom. Where appropriate, additional suggestions on how or when to teach a skill are provided. After the notes section, the content is presented in the form of a Proactive Teaching interaction. This is where the lesson reads like a script, one you can edit accordingly to fit the age and developmental level of your students.

Proactive Teaching is an instructional strategy you can use to introduce new social skills to students, reinforce the skills they are learning and prepare them for future situations where they will need to use specific skills or behaviors. In a Proactive Teaching interaction, you begin by introducing the skill. Each les-

Posters for Elementary Grades

If you are an elementary-grade teacher or work with special-needs students, the CD also contains fourteen alternative posters that may be useful when teaching the following skills: Greeting Others, Following Instructions, Staying on Task, Getting the Teacher's Attention, Talking with Others (Contributing to Discussions/Joining in a Conversation), Listening, Asking for What You Want (Making a Request/Asking a Favor), Accepting "No" for an Answer, Accepting Criticism, Disagreeing, Giving Criticism (Making an Appropriate Complaint), Saying You're Sorry (Making an Apology), Giving Compliments and Accepting Compliments.

These posters use simpler language that makes it easier for some students to understand, learn and remember the individual skill and its steps. In some instances, the skill name has been simplified or shortened and the number of skill steps has been reduced. When using one of these alternative posters, we recommend teaching the lesson using the same simplified language so there is greater consistency and less confusion.

son gives you a technique, along with talking points, that will focus students' attention on the skill and help them understand its relevance in their lives.

After introducing students to the skill, explain its behavioral steps. (A poster for each skill and its steps can be reproduced using the enclosed CD. Post them in your classroom to remind students how to follow and use the skills.)

The behavioral steps are numbered in the sequence in which they are performed. Additional talking points are provided so you can explain or clarify certain behaviors for students, such as defining "calm and pleasant" or describing an empathy statement. After reviewing the skill steps, the Proactive Teaching interaction concludes when you give students a reason, or rationale, for using the skill. Multiple rationales are included with each lesson. You can use all of the rationales or pick and choose those that have the most relevance and meaning to your students. After a skill is introduced and its behavioral steps are explained and rationales provided, you can move on to activities that reinforce the lesson and teach students how, when, where and why to use a skill.

Role-Plays, Suggested Activities and Think Sheets

In our experience, role-play is an effective instructional tool for helping students, especially younger ones, practice a skill's behavioral steps in a safe, controlled environment. Several true-to-life role-play scenarios, representing a range of age and developmental levels, are included in each lesson. If any scenario is not relevant or age-appropriate for your classroom, you can modify it accordingly or decide not to use that role-play with your students.

While role-plays can be excellent practice, not all students consider them to be enjoyable learning activities. Some students, particularly in junior and senior high, may view role-play as embarrassing or an excuse to act out. They will intentionally engage in antics that distract from the learning, or they simply won't participate. If this is a concern for you, each lesson also includes "Suggested Activities" that you can use in conjunction with, or as a replacement for, role-play.

Each suggested activity corresponds to a specific subject area and illustrates a way for you to integrate a skill into an academic lesson plan, homework assignment or other classroom function that is part of the school day. This strategy is called "blended teaching" and is an effective way to introduce a skill when there is limited time to teach a lesson plan by itself. In addition, blended teaching helps students see how these abstract concepts work in the real world and are relevant to their lives. Again, you can modify any activity to match the content you are covering in class, or you can use an activity to develop your own ideas and create something entirely new.

Each lesson also includes a "Think Sheet" handout (which you can reproduce, along with the role-play scenarios, using the enclosed CD). The think sheets ask a series of questions that encourage students to reflect thoughtfully about how a skill applies to their lives in and outside of the classroom. In the elementary grades, you may want students to work in groups to answer the questions or discuss them aloud in class to aid understanding. With older students, the think sheets can be assigned as homework or used as a group activity or a conversation sheet for large-group discussion. However you choose to use the think sheets, they can be a logical way to wrap up your teaching and transition to another lesson or activity.

While think sheets are a valuable component in teaching social skills, you also can use them as a tool for correcting behavioral mistakes. When a student struggles with a particular skill or repeats the same misbehavior, you can have him or her redo the relevant think sheet(s). In this context, the "re-think sheet" is part of a negative consequence. Repeating the exercise helps reinforce a skill and your behavioral expectations. Additionally, the time and energy a student spends redoing the questionnaire may be enough of a consequence to motivate positive changes in behavior.

These lesson plans provide a simple and efficient way to teach essential social skills. As students acquire and use these skills, their behaviors will shift in healthier, more positive directions. This behavioral shift, while good for students, is equally advantageous for you. One obvious benefit: Fewer disruptions equal more time for instruction. In addition, these lessons can help you forge deeper connections with students, making it easier to work through and move past behavioral mistakes. And, most importantly, you can ultimately create a learning community where everyone gives and shows respect, feels emotionally secure, strives for the same goals and finds real success.

About the Authors

Midge Odermann Mougey, Ed.D., is the principal of Jefferson Elementary School in North Platte, Nebraska. She has led the successful implementation of Boys Town's classroom behavior management program (The Well-Managed Classroom) at Jefferson for ten years and has been training other schools in the program since 1993. Prior to her ten years of administrative leadership, Mougey was a classroom teacher at the elementary and middle school levels and spearheaded the creation of The Learning Center, an alternative senior high school in North Platte.

Jo C. Dillon is a team leader with Boys Town's Training, Evaluation and Certification Division. For nearly thirty years, she was a classroom teacher in Colorado, Iowa and Nebraska schools. Dillon co-authored *Tools*

for Teaching Social Skills in School and was a contributing author to *No Room for Bullies*. She also helped pilot Reading Is FAME®, a nationally recognized program that helps adolescents who read below their grade level.

Denise Pratt is an assistant program coordinator with Boys Town's Training, Evaluation and Certification Division. Her professional career includes work with residential treatment programs and as a high school guidance counselor and experiential educator. For the past eight years, she has helped schools develop more effective ways to manage student behavior. Pratt also co-authored *Tools for Teaching Social Skills in School* and was a contributing author to *No Room for Bullies*.

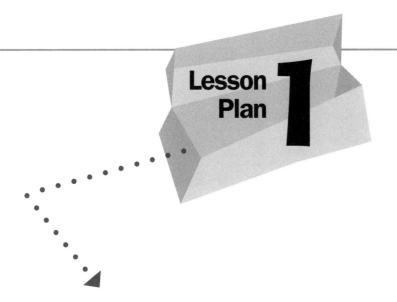

Greeting Others

Teacher Notes

"Greeting Others" is a skill that many teachers perceive as positive or somewhat helpful, but not critical to classroom management or student success. As a result, this skill is sometimes ignored completely or relegated to an afterthought. However, many learning communities report that when positive greetings are taught, modeled and used regularly, the social climate of classrooms and schools improves. Therefore, it can be highly advantageous for you to teach this skill at the start of the academic year rather than pushing it back or discounting it entirely.

As you describe the specific behavioral steps, remember to model the nonverbal behaviors or "paraskills" (eye contact, voice tone and body language) you want to see from students. Demonstrate what a "pleasant" or "sincere" voice sounds like, what a relaxed or confident body posture looks like and any other nonverbal behaviors that complement the skill steps.

Proactive Teaching Interaction

Introduce the Skill

Have your students brainstorm reasons why greeting others appropriately is important. Reasons can include:

- Shows pleasant personality
- Others see you as friendly
- Helps you make a good first impression
- Fosters a positive, warm environment

- Enhances morale
- Helps build and maintain a positive school culture
- Improves one's mood, or the moods of others

Describe the Appropriate Behavior or Skill Steps

Greeting Others

1. **Look at the person.**
   - Eye contact is a nonverbal behavior that helps communicate confidence, respect and maturity.

2. **Use a pleasant voice tone.**
   - An energetic or happy tone communicates to others that you are glad to meet them.

3. **Offer a verbal greeting.**
   - "Good morning" or "Good afternoon."
   - "Hello."
   - "Hi!"

Give a Reason or Rationale

A first impression is often a lasting one. This is why it is so important to know how to greet others in a friendly manner. By following the behavioral steps of "Greeting Others," you show that you are friendly, confident and positive. Additional benefits of using this skill appropriately include:

- You start new relationships on a positive note.
- You meet more people and potentially make more friends when you initiate a greeting.
- You leave a positive impression with others, which is essential in situations such as job interviews.
- You can ease the discomfort felt in unfamiliar situations, allowing you and others to feel more relaxed.
- Others will see you as mature, warm and friendly – just the kind of person they want to be around in the classroom, at home or at work.

Suggested Activities

Language Arts: Select a short story with a plot that takes place in a foreign country or has characters from non-English speaking nations. Have students research how people from those countries offer greetings. Examples can include "Bonjour," "Buenas Tardes," and "Guten Tag."

Science/Math: Provide students with a list of famous scientists and mathematicians and include general biographical information (nationality, years lived, famous discoveries, etc.). Have students review the list and familiarize themselves with the biographies. Write each scientist's and mathematician's name on separate nametags and give them to the students. Ask students to be the person whose name is written on the nametag and walk around the room greeting and introducing themselves to others.

For an added twist, you can put some of the nametags on the backs of some students, so they don't know who they are. Others in the class can introduce themselves and provide clues to these students, who then have to figure out which scientist or mathematician they are supposed to be.

History/Social Studies: When American presidents make official visits to foreign countries, their welcoming ceremonies are often elaborate celebrations that highlight the native dress, music and customs of the host country. Have students find articles and pictures of a U.S. president or other government dignitary being welcomed to a foreign land and discuss how that ceremony would look or sound different if the host country's leader was formally welcomed to the United States.

Greeting Others
Suggested Role-Plays

Teacher Note:
Have students select one of the following scenarios to role-play in class.

1. As you walk into the school building, you see the principal standing at the door. Offer a friendly greeting, and say the principal's name.

2. Walking down the hallway, you see a group of your friends. Following the steps of the skill, show how you would greet them in a friendly way.

3. You come home from school and see that your grandmother is visiting. Give her a friendly greeting.

4. A teacher you do not like very much walks into the classroom, and you are the only one there. Show how you would make him or her feel welcome by offering a friendly greeting.

5. You are not a morning person, and it's hard for you to be friendly early in the day. A teacher notices you enter the school, smiles at you and says, "Good morning!" Be friendly and greet the teacher.

Greeting Others
Think Sheet

Name_____ Date_____

What should "eye contact" look like?

- ❏ Looking someone in the eye and never looking away
- ❏ Looking someone in the eye and occasionally looking away
- ❏ Looking at someone's face
- ❏ Looking away most of the time, but making eye contact occasionally
- ❏ Facing the person who is talking to you

Why is it nice or helpful to look at the person whom you are greeting?

List some times when greeting others is important:

- ▪
- ▪
- ▪
- ▪

Brainstorm some friendly and respectful greetings that you can say to friends, teachers and other students:

How does the skill of **Greeting Others** help you at school?

Greeting Others

1. Look at the person.

2. Use a pleasant voice tone.

3. Offer a verbal greeting.

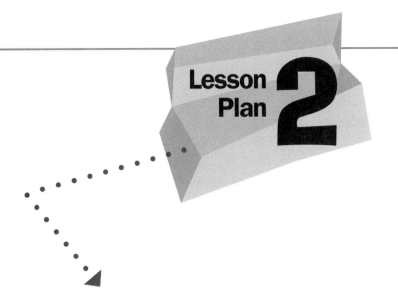

Setting Goals

Teacher Notes

Helping students prepare for their future is an important part of teaching, but it is often difficult. Young people tend to focus on the moment or what's going on this week rather than pondering what they want to become or achieve in the next week, month or year.

By helping students learn how to set goals for themselves, you can focus their energy in positive directions and encourage behaviors that will lead them to their goals. Students who have goals and are determined to achieve them are less likely to act out, give up or do something that could jeopardize their dreams.

Proactive Teaching Interaction

Introduce the Skill

Have students give examples of goals that apply to different aspects of their lives. Examples can include sports (running a six-minute mile), work (being on time every day for a month), social life (spending more time with friends), health (losing ten pounds in two months) or school (improving math grade from a "B" to an "A").

You also can have students brainstorm reasons why goal setting is important. Reasons can include:

- Gives you a practical plan for getting what you want
- Provides you with a sense of purpose and direction
- Helps you achieve your dreams

Describe the Appropriate Behavior or Skill Steps

Setting Goals

1. **Decide on your overall values and lifestyle desires.**

   - Think about and answer these questions: Where do I want to go in life? What kind of person do I want to be? What kind of friendships do I want? What kind of job or career do I want to pursue?

2. **List the resources you need to fulfill these lifestyle options.**

   - Create a mental inventory of the people, materials or organizations that can help you make your goals more attainable.

3. **Examine the intermediate steps in accomplishing your overall outcome.**

   - If your goal is to attend an Ivy League school, for example, find out what the admittance requirements are so you know what courses and tests to take and what extracurricular activities can give you the right credentials.

4. **Establish short- and long-term goals that will help you accomplish the steps necessary for the desired outcome.**

   - You can use short-term and long-term goals as steps to help you reach an overall or ultimate objective. For example, if your overall goal is to graduate from eighth grade to ninth grade (or graduate high school), a short-term goal would be to complete all of your assignments and readings on time every week. This short-term goal will help you attain the long-term goal of earning passing grades. By passing all of your classes, you can graduate and attain your ultimate objective.

   - Short-term goals and long-term goals also can be separate from each other. A short-term goal can relate to anything you want to achieve in the near future, such as completing a book report by the end of the week. A long-term goal usually involves more time, such as losing ten pounds in eight weeks.

Give a Reason or Rationale

Setting goals helps give your life direction and can motivate you to learn and do more. Goals also can provide you with a sense of purpose and a reason for doing things that you may otherwise never do. Other benefits of goal setting include:

■ Others see you as a hard worker and success-oriented.

■ You develop perseverance, patience and character working toward goals.

■ You enjoy a sense of relief, accomplishment and pride when you attain your goals.

Suggested Activities

Language Arts: Have students practice completing various college or work applications. Have students create a sample resume with a cover letter that describes their immediate and long-term goals.

Social Studies: Give students copies, or listen to a recording, of Dr. Martin Luther King, Jr.'s *I Have a Dream* speech. Have students create a symbol that represents their interpretation of his dream for America. Discuss what long-term goal he sought and what laws, actions or movements (short-term goals) needed to happen before that vision could be realized. Ask students to discuss or debate whether or not more needs to be done to fulfill Dr. King's dream.

Other significant moments or movements in history can be discussed, such as the space program and moon landing. Have students identify the short-term and long-term goals, including any setbacks that occurred. Ask students to explain how goal setting was a necessary component in achieving success.

Science/Math: Plan a school beautification project to spruce up the school grounds or the common areas inside the building by planting, transplanting or potting flowers, shrubs, grasses and trees. Have students create a plan for where and when to plant, based on sunlight, moisture, available space, growing season and lifecycle. The plan also should include a completion date and short-term objectives related to the purchase, planting, care and maintenance of the plants.

Physical Education: Have students develop a diet and exercise program to increase their fitness level. Include a long-term goal (total weight loss or gain, run five miles, etc.) that is safe and realistic. Each student's program should have at least five short-term goals to help measure progress toward the overall goal and include specifics about the diet and exercise routine for a two-week period.

Setting Group Goals

Goal setting is oftentimes a highly personal and individualized skill. To practice and reinforce the skill steps, we recommend selecting a goal that students can work toward achieving together and that addresses an issue or problem that is relevant to your learning community.

Start by identifying a problem that students need to improve, and then set a goal to overcome or correct the problem. Clearly label what goal you want to achieve and establish clear behavioral expectations to achieve the goal. In this scenario, the goal is to have students tidy up the classroom and be more organized at the end of a class period.

Goal: Leave the classroom tidy, and take everything you need with you.

1. During the last two minutes of class, clean your desk/work station.

2. Gather all of your books, notes and materials.

3. Put your homework in your assignment folder.

4. Straighten your desk/push your chair in.

Other classroom/school goals can focus on reducing tardiness, increasing acts of kindness or improving attendance.

Setting Goals
Think Sheet

Name_____ Date_____

Your goal for this school year is…

Is this goal possible? Why or why not?

What time limit do you have to reach this goal?

What steps do you need to follow to reach your goal?

List any problems or obstacles that might keep you from reaching your goal:

-

-

-

-

How can you get past each of the problems or obstacles you listed above?

-

-

-

-

Who can help you reach your goal, and how?

What or who will keep you motivated to reach your goal?

How will you know when you reach your goal?

Setting Goals

1. **Decide on your overall values and lifestyle desires.**

2. **List the resources you need to fulfill these lifestyle options.**

3. **Examine the intermediate steps in accomplishing your overall outcome.**

4. **Establish short- and long-term goals that will help you accomplish the steps necessary for the desired outcome.**

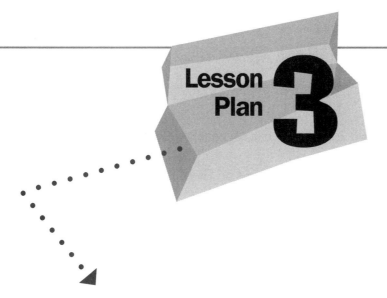

Being Prepared for Class

Teacher Notes

Perhaps the biggest cause for delay and unnecessary distraction in the classroom is unprepared students. These individuals never seem to have the right books, or they frequently forget supplies or spend the first several minutes of every class period socializing and loafing about. While some of this behavior may be attributable to a student's laid-back attitude or personality, that's not a sufficient reason to excuse or ignore the behavior.

One strategy to help students overcome their tendency to be disorganized is to teach them how to be responsible. This skill lesson provides a concrete way to teach students about responsibility. Many unnecessary classroom delays or disruptions will fade away if students can become more responsible, and you will be rewarded with more instruction time.

Proactive Teaching Interaction

Introduce the Skill

Start a class discussion by asking students to define what it means to be prepared for class. Have students give examples of being prepared for your class and not being prepared. After the discussion, ask students to brainstorm reasons why it is important for them to use this skill. Reasons can include:

■ Keeps the class on schedule by eliminating delays that cut into instruction time

■ Gives you more time in class to read, complete assignments or work on projects

■ Makes class less stressful

■ Sets a good example for others

■ Keeps you out of trouble, avoids negative consequences

Describe the Appropriate Behavior or Skill Steps

Being Prepared for Class

1. **Gather all necessary books, papers, homework and writing implements.**

   ▪ Make sure you have a sharpened pencil or pen that works.

2. **Be on time for class.**

   ▪ This usually means you are sitting at your desk and ready to work when the bell rings or class begins.

3. **Present homework and assignments when the teacher asks for them.**

4. **Write down assignments and homework to complete.**

   ▪ Use an assignment notebook or folder to write down or hold the assignments you're given, and remember to take the notebook or folder home with you every day.

Give a Reason or Rationale

Being prepared for class is essential to your academic success. When you show up on time, have your materials and are attentive, it's much easier to stay on task and gather all of the information you need. If you're always coming late to class or forgetting your notes and assignments, you are much more likely to be distracted (and be a distraction), miss critical information and earn penalties for tardiness or late assignments. Other benefits of being prepared for class include:

■ You can apply this skill to work settings, making you a more valuable employee.

■ You avoid the embarrassment of always having to ask others to share their books and supplies with you in class.

■ You are less likely to fall behind, especially in fast-paced and heavy-content courses.

■ You develop a reputation as someone who is responsible and dependable.

Suggested Activities

Language Arts: Write the poem *Preparation* by Paul Dunbar on an overhead or the board. Read the poem aloud, and then ask students to interpret its meaning.

Have students write an original poem using preparation as their theme.

Preparation

The little bird sits in the nest and sings
A shy, soft song to the morning light;
And it flutters a little and prunes its wings.
The song is halting and poor and brief,
And the fluttering wings scarce stir a leaf;
But the note is a prelude to sweeter things,
And the busy bill and the flutter slight
Are proving the wings for a bolder flight!

History: Preparation can be the difference between great success and complete failure. Have students prepare a written or oral report about an historical event or program that succeeded or failed because of the planning. Examples can include the D-Day invasion, Marshall Plan, Bay of Pigs, etc.

Group Role-Play

In addition to individual role-play scenarios, this skill lends itself to large-group role-play. Specifically, you can design a role-play around how you want your students to come prepared to your classroom. Start by creating a procedure that describes the behavior expectations you have for coming prepared to class, and then have students practice the procedure. Here are two examples:

Coming Prepared to Class
- Have all of your materials with you when entering the classroom.
- Go directly to your seat.
- Get your materials out and put them on your desk.
- Sit quietly while the teacher gives instructions.

What to Do if You're Late to Class
- Go to the office (or back to the previous teacher).
- Use a pleasant voice.
- Request a pass to class.
- Walk to class.
- Enter quietly.
- Give the pass to the teacher.
- Take your seat quietly.

Being Prepared for Class
Suggested Role-Plays

Teacher Note:

Have students select one of the following scenarios to role-play in class.

1. On Friday, your teacher tells you to come to class on Monday with two stories from a local newspaper and one story from any news magazine. Say or describe what you need to do to remember this assignment over the weekend, and what you need to do Monday to show your teacher that you are ready for class.

2. On Monday, your teacher tells you there will be an open-book test on Wednesday. You also will be able to use your class notes. Show or describe what you need to do so you are ready for the test.

3. Next week, your gym class is going to a local swimming pool. Transportation will be provided and there is no fee. However, you are responsible for anything else you might need. Describe what you have to do to be prepared for next week's gym class.

Being Prepared for Class
Think Sheet

Name_____ Date_____

What does being prepared for class mean or look like when you are going to…

- band class?

- physical education class?

- science class?

Why is it important to know how to be prepared for class?

How does the skill of **Being Prepared for Class** help you at school?

How can you use the skill of **Being Prepared for Class** to do a chore at home, volunteer in the community or hold a job?

Being Prepared for Class

1. Gather all necessary books, papers, homework and writing implements.

2. Be on time for class.

3. Present homework and assignments when the teacher asks for them.

4. Write down assignments and homework to complete.

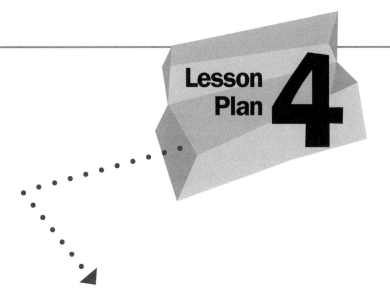

Following Instructions

Teacher Notes

The ability to follow instructions is a fundamental skill that students need in the classroom, at home, at work, on the athletic field and in any extracurricular activity. Because it is so essential to classroom management, you should introduce this skill on the first day of class and frequently review it throughout the first week of school.

For older students (middle and high school), this skill may seem too elementary. However, when teaching a basic skill such as this one, your emphasis should be on helping these students learn "code switching." Code switching is when students can successfully alter the behavioral steps of a skill to best adapt to or reflect the different circumstances and relationships they encounter (saying "Yeah" and nodding "Yes" rather than saying "Okay") without diminishing a skill's effectiveness.

Proactive Teaching Interaction

Introduce the Skill

Introduce the skill by having students complete a learning activity that requires them to follow specific instructions, such as an origami exercise, classroom treasure hunt or a multi-step drawing activity.

You also can brainstorm reasons why it is important to know how to follow instructions. Reasons can include:

- Shows maturity
- Saves time

■ Makes it more likely projects get done correctly the first time

■ Helps create a smooth-running classroom or activity

Describe the Appropriate Behavior or Skill Steps

Following Instructions

1. **Look at the person.**

   ▪ Eye contact is important because it communicates confidence, makes the other person feel engaged and focuses your attention on the individual.

   ▪ Maintain a pleasant facial expression.

2. **Say "Okay," and/or nod to show understanding.**

   ▪ "Understanding" means you comprehend the instruction or direction. Saying "Okay" indicates that you know what is expected or needs to be done, even if it is something you may not want to do.

   ▪ You can communicate your understanding by using various nonverbal cues, such as:

     ▫ Smiling

     ▫ Giving a "thumbs up"

     ▫ Giving the "Okay" hand sign

3. **Do what you've been asked right away.**

   ▪ "Right away" means within a few seconds after hearing an instruction.

   ▪ Complete the entire task.

   ▪ Do the task accurately.

   ▪ Stay on task.

   ▪ Do the best that you can.

4. **Check back. (This step can be optional.)**

   ▪ "Checking back" may be necessary if you are given an instruction from someone who cannot observe you complete the task. Examples include when a teacher asks you to take papers to the principal's office or when your parent asks you to clean the garage.

   ▪ What other situations can you name where it is important to check back?

Give a Reason or Rationale

To be successful in school, athletics, work, family life and friendships, you need to know how to follow instructions correctly. Knowing how to follow instructions has many benefits:

- When you do what you're told to do right away, parents and teachers will be more likely to praise you or be happy about your effort.

- You can finish assignments or jobs sooner, allowing you more time for other activities.

- You can learn necessary skills more quickly, giving you more opportunities or promotions at work or in school.

- Teachers, employers and even your parents won't ask you to redo your work as often, and you will develop a reputation for being mature, responsible and competent.

- You will make a positive contribution to your school, family, job and community, which can boost your confidence and sense of self.

Suggested Activities

Language Arts: Teach and reinforce the skill of "Following Instructions" by linking it to a specific academic task or what is going on in your classroom. For example, prior to beginning a read-aloud, give students explicit instructions for the activity: open books to a specific page, follow along with the reading, be prepared to read aloud when your name is called, remain silent when others are reading and raise your hand if you do not understand a concept or know the meaning of a word. After the exercise, discuss how well everyone followed the instructions and what, if any, improvements need to be made.

You also can ask students to search for news stories about individuals who did not follow instructions and the consequences that resulted. Have students read their stories aloud and then discuss what lessons can be learned. Story examples can include workers or managers not following safety procedures at industrial plants or patients not following the instructions on their prescription medication bottles.

Family and Consumer Sciences: Have students plan and cater a school or community food event. Instruct students to create a multi-course meal with hors d'oeuvres, breads, salads, soups, entrees and desserts. Assign groups to be responsible for selecting the menu, preparing the food, serving the guests and decorating the site. The plan should include responsibilities and guidelines to follow that are related to timelines, budget and attire. Do a post-event assessment to evaluate how well students complied with the event guidelines, including following recipes, meeting deadlines and managing the budget.

Science/Math: During a dissection unit (frogs, worms, etc.), have students work in lab groups. Provide a list of steps or directions that all the groups must follow during the dissection process. Have each group perform one step at its lab station, and then move to another station to perform the next step and so on. Continue to rotate the groups until the dissections are complete. Afterward, discuss how well each group followed the steps. If a group failed to follow a direction, talk about the effect it had on groups that followed it at that station.

Following Instructions
Suggested Role-Plays

Teacher Note:
Have students select one of the following scenarios to role-play in class.

1. Your teacher asks you to pick up a piece of litter and put it in the trash bin. Show how you would follow the instructions correctly.

2. The principal asks you to come to the office. Look at the principal with a pleasant facial expression, say "Okay" and immediately walk to the office.

3. Your teacher tells the entire class to take out their history books, open them to page 47 and start reading. Show how you would follow those instructions.

4. Your mom asks you to clear the table after dinner. Describe what you would do to complete this task.

5. A substitute teacher asks you to take roll. Show how this should look.

Following Instructions
Think Sheet

Name_____ Date_____

Why is it important to know how to follow instructions?

List some times when following instructions is very important:

-
-
-
-

When you are given an instruction, how soon should you follow it at…

school?

home?

work?

How does the skill of **Following Instructions** help you at school?

How does the skill of **Following Instructions** help you at home?

Following Instructions

1. Look at the person.

2. Say "Okay," and/or nod to show understanding.

3. Do what you've been asked right away.

4. Check back. (This step can be optional.)

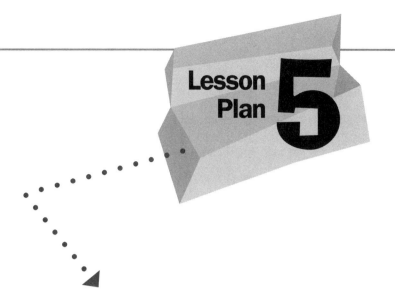

Lesson Plan 5

Staying on Task

Teacher Notes

There will always be distractions for students – friends, school activities, external events, hunger, boredom, fatigue, etc. Those who cannot maintain their focus amid the external commotion and internal turmoil or get back on task quickly can suffer academically: Assignments get turned in late or unfinished; time expires before all test questions get answered; and individual and group projects get delayed. When students are off task, unruly and inappropriate behaviors are more likely and your learning community becomes more chaotic for everyone.

Proactive Teaching Interaction

Introduce the Skill

Ask students to describe common classroom and school distractions that interrupt their studies. List their responses on the board, and then ask them to brainstorm strategies for coping with those distractions. Also, have students explain why it is important to know how to stay on task. Reasons can include:

- Allows work to get done sooner
- Keeps you from distracting others
- Decreases the amount of work you have to take home
- Increases productivity

Describe the Appropriate Behavior or Skill Steps

Staying on Task

1. **Look at your task or assignment.**

   - Don't procrastinate or put it away for "later."

2. **Think about the steps needed to complete the task.**

   - Consider what materials (textbook, pens, calculator, etc.) or information (facts, dates, class notes, etc.) you need.

3. **Focus all of your attention on the task.**

   - Keep your eyes on your own work.

4. **Stop working only when instructed.**

   - Follow the teacher's instructions.

5. **Ignore distractions and interruptions from others.**

   - Don't interrupt or be a distraction to others.

Give a Reason or Rationale

In school, you are expected to complete assignments, quizzes and other projects in a timely manner. Knowing how to stay on task can help you get your work done correctly and on time. Other benefits of staying on task include:

- You manage your time better and have more opportunities to do other things.

- You don't distract or disrupt others from their work.

- You contribute to a positive learning environment.

- You show your teachers, parents and peers that you are responsible and take projects seriously.

Suggested Activities

Language Arts: Have students read Scott O'Dell's *Island of the Blue Dolphins* (grades 3-6), Jules Feiffer's *The Man in the Ceiling* (grades 3-6), Mildred D. Taylor's *Roll of Thunder, Hear My Cry* (grades 7-10) or any age-appropriate novel about perseverance and not giving up. Have them write short essays identifying examples of a character staying on task, and how the character was rewarded for persevering.

Science/Math: Have students research significant architectural achievements (Mount Rushmore, Panama Canal, etc.) or inventors and their inventions

(Thomas Edison and the light bulb, Dr. Patricia E. Bath and the Laserphaco Probe, etc.). Lead a discussion about how the skill of "Staying on Task" helped individuals overcome obstacles and maintain focus in pursuit of their goals.

History/Government: Have students research the women's suffrage movement, from the Seneca Falls Convention in 1848 to the ratification of the 19th Amendment in 1920. Lead a discussion about the types of challenges and opposition women such as Elizabeth Cady Stanton, Lucretia Mott and Susan B. Anthony confronted in the fight for voting rights. Have students explain how staying on task relates to that seven-decade struggle.

Staying on Task
Suggested Role-Plays

Teacher Note:

Have students select one of the following scenarios to role-play in class.

1. Your best friend keeps asking you questions as you are trying to finish your math sheet. Show or say how you would stay on task.

2. As you give an oral book report in front of the class, you hear some classmates whispering. Show or say how you would stay focused on giving your report.

3. During study hall, you are working on an English assignment when a friend passes you a note. Following the steps of the skill, show how you would ignore the note and concentrate on your assignment.

4. You are studying for tomorrow's big test when you get several text messages from your friends. Show or say how you would ignore the messages and stay focused on your studies.

5. Your history assignment is to have Chapter 5 read by tomorrow. You are trying to read in the living room, where your mom and dad are visiting and watching the news. Show or describe how you would ignore the distractions and focus on your reading.

6. During the spelling bee, two classmates are making faces at you while you are trying to spell a word. Show or say how you would ignore them.

Staying on Task
Think Sheet

Name_____ Date_____

Why is it important to know how to stay on task?

What are some things you can do to stay on task at school?

- ▪

- ▪

- ▪

- ▪

How does the skill of **Staying on Task** help you at school?

How does the skill of **Staying on Task** help you at home?

When you stay on task, why is that helpful to your teacher and classmates?

Staying on Task

1. **Look at your task or assignment.**

2. **Think about the steps needed to complete the task.**

3. **Focus all of your attention on the task.**

4. **Stop working only when instructed.**

5. **Ignore distractions and interruptions from others.**

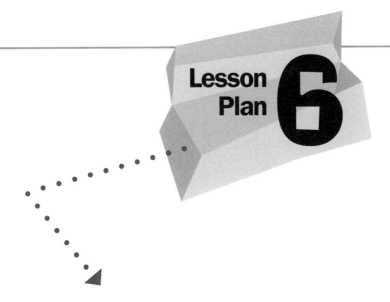

Getting the Teacher's Attention

Teacher Notes

Similar to the skill of "Greeting Others," teaching students how to get your attention in an appropriate way is a basic skill that should be taught at the start of the academic year and reviewed often.

One frustration teachers experience in the classroom is when students blurt out comments or answers, interrupting instruction time. Research suggests that it takes, on average, 18 to 24 months for students to internalize a skill. In other words, they make the skill part of their routine and can use it consistently. Although students can learn the steps of a skill quickly, patience is required. Some students will struggle to remember to use a skill, especially when stressed or excited. It's important to keep in mind that learning is a process, not a singular event.

Proactive Teaching Interaction

Introduce the Skill

You can teach and reinforce this skill in the classroom throughout the school day, if necessary. Have students practice the skill by raising their hands, waiting their turns to be called on and asking questions or making statements in a calm manner.

Have students brainstorm reasons why it is important to know how to get a teacher's attention appropriately. Reasons can include:

- Decreases noise level
- Shows respect to others

- Helps keep others on task
- Limits disruptions during lessons and activities

Describe the Appropriate Behavior or Skill Steps

Getting the Teacher's Attention

1. **Look at the teacher.**
   - Maintain eye contact.

2. **Raise your hand calmly.**
   - Do not pump your fist in the air or frantically wave your arm back and forth.

3. **Wait to be acknowledged by the teacher.**
   - Don't assume the teacher is coming to you first; wait to speak until spoken to.

4. **Ask questions or make requests in a calm voice.**
   - Don't whine or scream; use a quiet voice.

Give a Reason or Rationale

Knowing how to get a teacher's attention appropriately helps create an orderly and well-managed classroom. The less chaotic the classroom, the more opportunities you and your classmates will have to ask questions, get help and learn. Other benefits of knowing how to get a teacher's attention include:

- You show respect to your teacher and others in the classroom.
- You contribute to a positive, orderly classroom environment.
- You are more likely to get quicker answers to your questions and requests.
- You help the teacher know that you have a problem or need help.

Suggested Activities

Language Arts: Have students reflect on experiences from their own lives to write a fictional short story about people going to extraordinary lengths to get attention for themselves or a cause they are supporting. Ask for volunteers to read their stories aloud, and then discuss whether the actions described in the story were appropriate or not, and why.

Social Studies: Lead a discussion about how organizations and individuals sometimes use controversial tactics to bring attention to themselves or their causes. Have students find examples of protests or campaigns that were done to create public awareness, and then debate their effectiveness. Examples can include civil rights marches, PETA (People for the Ethical Treatment of Animals) demonstrations, street protests or acts of civil disobedience (environmentalists chaining themselves to trees, consumers boycotting genetically engineered foods, etc.).

Getting the
Teacher's Attention
Suggested Role-Plays

Teacher Note:
Have students select one of the following scenarios to role-play in class.

1. You do not understand the instructions on your worksheet. Following the steps of the skill, show how you would gain the teacher's attention and ask for help.

2. Your teacher told everyone to raise their hands when they finished their exams, and she would pick them up. You are not finished with your test, but you need help with one of the essay questions. Show how you would handle this situation.

3. Your teacher is verbally quizzing your class about a reading assignment. You know the answers to many of the questions. Show how to properly get the teacher's attention.

4. To leave your seat during study hall, you need to get permission from the study hall monitor. Following the steps of the skill, show how to get the monitor's attention, and then ask for a hall pass so you can go to the restroom.

Getting the Teacher's Attention
Think Sheet

Name _____ Date _____

Why is it important to know how to get a teacher's attention without being loud or distracting?

How does the skill of **Getting the Teacher's Attention** help you in the classroom?

List some times when the skill of **Getting the Teacher's Attention** is very important:

-

-

-

-

How can the skill of **Getting the Teacher's Attention** be used in situations that involve other adults outside of school? How would you change this skill to fit this new setting?

Getting the Teacher's Attention

1. **Look at the teacher.**

2. **Raise your hand calmly.**

3. **Wait to be acknowledged by the teacher.**

4. **Ask questions or make requests in a calm voice.**

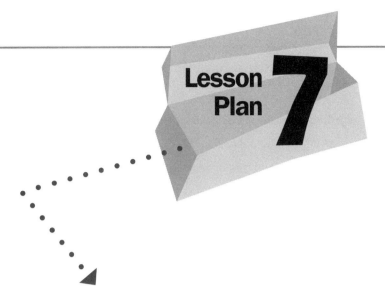

Contributing to Discussions (Joining in a Conversation)

Teacher Notes

This skill is particularly helpful for students who are shy or lack the confidence to answer questions aloud or share their ideas in class. Because students can often earn extra credit for participation, it's important that they acquire and use this skill throughout their academic careers.

As a teacher, it's also important for you to create a classroom environment that is welcoming and respectful. Students who possess this skill may still be unwilling to participate if they fear being mocked or ridiculed by others when they speak up.

Proactive Teaching Interaction

Introduce the Skill

Ask students if they ever joined a conversation with people who were not close friends. If any say yes, ask them to describe how they joined in and what they said. Continue the discussion by asking students if they ever refused to join, or remained silent during, a conversation. Have them describe the situation and the reason(s) why they did not participate.

After sharing stories, brainstorm reasons why it is important to know how to contribute to a discussion or join a conversation. Reasons can include:

- Others learn your opinions and thoughts
- Helps you learn what others believe or think

- Shows interest in people and ideas
- Encourages relationships and friendships
- Allows you to correct misunderstandings or answer questions
- Can be fun and enlightening

Describe the Appropriate Behavior or Skill Steps

Contributing to Discussions (Joining in a Conversation)

1. **Look at the people who are talking.**

   - Eye contact communicates interest and engagement.

2. **Wait for a point when no one else is talking.**

   - You can build on something that someone else said by adding your perspective. An example would be saying something like, "I agree with Sarah, but I also noticed…."

3. **Make a short, appropriate comment that relates to the topic being discussed.**

   - Don't dominate a discussion; give others time to speak.

4. **Choose words that will not be offensive or confusing to others.**

5. **Give other people a chance to participate.**

   - If you notice someone hasn't had a chance to speak, encourage his or her participation by saying something like, "What do you think about…?"

Give a Reason or Rationale

Communication is an essential part of the school day. As a student, you need to know how to discuss issues with your classmates, teachers, administrators and others in the classroom and outside the learning community. By knowing how to contribute to discussions, you can let others know how you feel and make it easier for others to communicate with you. Other benefits of knowing how to contribute to discussions include:

- You learn what other people think and feel about issues.
- You build relationships and make friendships because you engage with others and share experiences.
- You can learn things you didn't know.
- In the classroom, you might earn extra points for participation.

Suggested Activities

Language Arts: Write the following quote from George Bernard Shaw on the board or overhead. Read the quote aloud, and then ask students to identify the skill steps that most relate to the quote. Also ask students to explain what it means to lose the art of conversation but not the power of speech.

"She had lost the art of conversation, but not, unfortunately, the power of speech."

Science/Math: Have students debate or discuss issues or topics related to science and engineering. Start by writing questions or topics on individual flashcards (explain why the sky is blue, explain how to compute a differentiation formula, discuss the Heisenberg Principle, etc.). Divide students into groups of three or four, and have each group pick a card. One at a time, have the groups come to the front of the class and debate or discuss the topic written on the flashcard for a set period of time (three to five minutes). Encourage students to follow the steps of the skill to have a good discussion. This activity also can be a useful review prior to unit exams.

History: During a unit on World War I or World War II, conduct a classroom peace conference, with students representing each of the countries involved in the conflict. Configure the classroom so students can sit in a circle or semi-circle. Have students debate or discuss the terms of a peace treaty. Before any peace deal can be ratified, every representative at the table must contribute to the discussion.

Contributing to Discussions (Joining in a Conversation)
Suggested Role-Plays

Teacher Note:

Have students select one of the following scenarios to role-play in class.

1. At a family reunion, you overhear two cousins talking about one of your favorite movies. Following the steps of the skill, show how you would join their discussion.

2. During recess, a group of students is talking about their favorite school lunch menus. Show how you would let them know what your favorite foods are.

3. In geography class, your teacher asks students to share anything they want about their favorite city in the state. Show how you would participate in the class discussion and include what you would say about your favorite city.

4. While standing at your locker, you hear a group of older students talking about their favorite reality TV show. You think the show is great, too. Show how you would join their conversation.

5. Your parents invited friends over for dinner. At the dining table, two of them talk about a restaurant they really like. You do not know anything about the restaurant. Show or describe how you would join their conversation so you can learn more about the restaurant and its food.

Contributing to Discussions (Joining in a Conversation)
Think Sheet

Name_____ Date_____

Why is it important to know how to contribute to discussions and join conversations?

One step of the skill is to make a short, appropriate comment about the topic being discussed. What is an appropriate thing to say when the topic is about…

tomorrow's math quiz?

today's lunch menu?

the town's new aquatic park?

a friend's summer vacation?

tonight's big game?

How does the skill of **Contributing to Discussions (Joining in a Conversation)** help you in the classroom?

How does the skill of **Contributing to Discussions (Joining in a Conversation)** help you at home or work?

Contributing to Discussions
(Joining in a Conversation)

1. Look at the people who are talking.

2. Wait for a point when no one else is talking.

3. Make a short, appropriate comment that relates to the topic being discussed.

4. Choose words that will not be offensive or confusing to others.

5. Give other people a chance to participate.

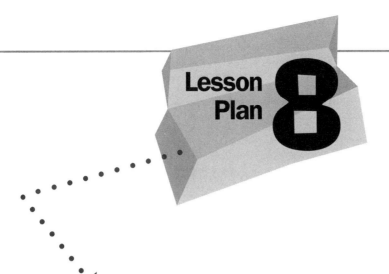

Listening to Others

Teacher Notes

"Listening to Others" is a useful skill for all students, but especially for those who are easily distracted. Students who know how to listen are much more likely to understand directions, learn new material and have better social relationships.

Proactive Teaching Interaction

Introduce the Skill

Begin this lesson with an activity that encourages students to listen intently. Read a passage from a book or an article from a newspaper, and then ask students to recall names of characters, facts or main ideas from the reading.

You also can have students brainstorm reasons why it is important to know how to listen to others. Reasons can include:

- Keeps you informed
- Shows respect
- Demonstrates openness to hear new ideas or different opinions

Describe the Appropriate Behavior or Skill Steps

Listening to Others

1. **Look at the person who is talking and remain quiet.**

   - Maintain eye contact.

2. **Wait until the person is finished talking before you speak.**

    - Be respectful; don't interrupt or walk away.

3. **Show that you heard the person by nodding your head and saying "Okay" or "That's interesting."**

    - Verbal responses may not always be necessary, especially when you are in a large group.

Give a Reason or Rationale

Listening to what others say is a valuable skill at home, in school and on the job. Being an active listener helps you learn new things, understand what others are asking or telling you to do and shows respect to the speaker. In everyday life, good listening skills allow you to develop friendships, maintain relationships, accept feedback and expand your knowledge. Knowing how to listen to others has many other benefits:

- You increase the likelihood of acquiring the information you need to be successful in school or on the job.

- You appear competent because you know what's going on around you, and others will see you as a leader.

- When it's your turn to speak, others will be more willing to listen to you.

- You look attentive and respectful, and adults value those qualities in students.

Suggested Activities

Language Arts: Play a portion of an audio book in class. Stop the recording and ask students to take out a sheet of paper and write down as many facts and details that they can recall. Give them a few minutes to record their answers, and then have them put down their pencils. Play a second, longer segment of the audio book. After you stop the recording, again ask students to write down as many details as they can remember. When they're done, have students exchange their notes with others in the class. See who recalled the most information accurately, and discuss the challenges they experienced while listening to the audio book.

Science/Math: In science, new discoveries, technologies and areas of research often create controversies outside the scientific community. Issues such as cloning, embryonic stem cell research, eugenics, global warming and space exploration can galvanize individuals to enthusiastically support or oppose specific programs and legislation. Play a video clip from a news or television program where experts debate a controversial scientific subject. Ask students to write down the arguments they hear in support of, or in opposition to, a particular viewpoint. Have students share their answers aloud and discuss how many debate points they heard, missed or misunderstood. Questions to consider include: Did anyone interrupt or talk over someone else? Did anyone misquote or distort someone else's comments? Did the moderator have to repeat or rephrase questions, and why?

Listening to Others
Suggested Role-Plays

Teacher Note:

Have students select one of the following scenarios to role-play in class.

1. Your teacher is talking about tonight's homework assignment. Show how you would pay attention.

2. Your class welcomes a guest speaker to talk about the NASA shuttle program. Show how you would listen carefully to the speaker.

3. Your classmates are presenting their history projects. Show how you would listen to them.

4. Your school is having an all-day assembly with speakers and performers. Show how you would be respectful to the guests and interested in what they are saying and doing.

5. Your dad is telling you how to stack and clear dishes from the dining table. Show or say how you would listen carefully.

6. Your uncle is explaining the rules of a board game to you and a friend. Following the steps of the skill, show or describe how you would listen so your uncle wouldn't have to repeat the instructions.

Listening to Others
Think Sheet

Name _____ Date _____

List some places where being an active listener or listening carefully is important:

-

-

-

-

List some times when listening to others is very important:

-

-

-

-

What facial expressions (smiling, frowning, yawning, glaring, etc.) should you have when listening to others?

How does the skill of **Listening to Others** help you at school?

How does the skill of **Listening to Others** help you at home?

Listening to Others

1. **Look at the person who is talking and remain quiet.**

2. **Wait until the person is finished talking before you speak.**

3. **Show that you heard the person by nodding your head and saying "Okay" or "That's interesting."**

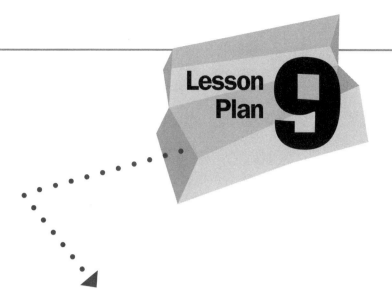

Completing Homework

Teacher Notes

A big issue for many educators is the problem of missing, late or incomplete homework. Not only does this problem undermine students' academic progress, but it also can disrupt how quickly and efficiently you progress through the content of your lesson plans. Many students who struggle with schoolwork do so because they never learned proper study habits, including how to do homework.

The ultimate responsibility for finishing homework on time falls on students. However, you can help them learn to be more responsible by teaching this skill. The skill incorporates practical steps that can make homework feel less daunting and overwhelming.

Proactive Teaching Interaction

Introduce the Skill

A logical time to introduce this skill is immediately prior to handing out homework assignments. Ask students why they think teachers assign homework and then discuss what type of assignments are their most and least favorite. Have students brainstorm reasons why it's important to complete homework. Reasons can include:

- Helps you learn a subject

- Reinforces a reading or lecture

- Allows the teacher to measure how well you understand the subject and decide if more instruction is needed

■ Prevents you from earning an incomplete

■ Teaches you how to use learning resources

■ Becomes a study aid when preparing for quizzes and exams

Describe the Appropriate Behavior or Skill Steps

Completing Homework

1. **Find out at school what the day's homework is for each subject.**

   ▪ Look on the board, check the class Web page or talk to the appropriate teachers or other students from your classes.

   ▪ Remember to follow the steps of "Making a Request (Asking a Favor)" when you ask others for information about homework.

2. **Remember to bring home necessary books or materials in order to complete your assignments.**

   ▪ Review your assignments and make a checklist of the books and resources needed.

3. **Get started on homework promptly, or at the designated time.**

   ▪ Be consistent. Set a study time (after or before dinner, etc.) and stick to it as often as you can.

   ▪ Have a designated spot to do homework that is free from distractions (television, text messages, cell phone, iPod, etc.).

4. **Complete all assignments accurately and neatly.**

   ▪ Stay on task until you complete the assignment.

   ▪ Ask a parent or sibling to review your work.

5. **Carefully store completed homework until the next school day.**

   ▪ Put assignments in a folder, notebook or backpack that you will remember to take to school.

Give a Reason or Rationale

Sometimes homework can seem like a drag because you would rather spend your time playing video games or talking with friends. Instead of looking at homework as a negative, try to see the positives. Homework is your opportunity to work independently and learn new things. When you complete assignments on time, you might improve your grades, too. Other benefits of doing homework include:

■ You have an opportunity to demonstrate what you know.

■ You will feel less stress in class because your work is done.

- You won't get in trouble with the teacher or your parents for late or incomplete work.
- Your grades might improve, earning you extra rewards at school or home.
- You learn to meet deadlines, which is a skill needed in most jobs.
- You develop better study habits.

Suggested Activities

As an educator, you naturally put students in situations that require them to use various social skills. In addition to blending social skill instruction with academic instruction, you also can incorporate the teaching of social skills with specific academic tasks, such as homework. The following examples highlight opportunities for teaching social skills based on what is happening in the classroom.

Language Arts: Prior to an exam, explain how you want students to prepare for the exam (review notes of class lectures, re-read chapter summaries in the textbook, review previous homework assignments and think about possible test questions and answers).

Science/Math: Prior to sending students into the lab, where they will work in pairs, explain how you want students to work together (assign responsibilities, speak quietly and work until the assignment is completed).

History: Prior to an in-class assignment, explain what you want students to do (use class textbook and lecture notes, work quietly, raise your hand if you have questions, turn your assignment sheet over when you are done and read silently or work on homework until everyone finishes).

Group Role-Play

Completing homework is another skill that is personal and highly individualized. For role-play, we recommend doing a group exercise that teaches students how to follow instructions, gather appropriate materials and complete an assignment accurately and completely in a specified amount of time.

Start by dividing the class into groups of three or four students and have each group work on completing an assignment. Choose an appropriate textbook (world history, science, social studies, etc.) and instruct each group to answer all of the review questions at the end of a specific chapter. Students should assign responsibilities to each group member ("readers" look for information in the chapter text, "researchers" search for additional information from outside sources – Internet, class notes, almanac, etc. – and "recorders" write down the answers). The length of time you give students to complete the assignment should be based on chapter length, the number and complexity of the questions and the amount of available class time you have.

You also can have students work in small groups to develop individual plans for completing their homework (when, where, etc.), and then use those plans to set an attainable goal for the class. For example, a class goal can be to have every student follow his or her plan and complete homework on time for one week. If the goal is met, students earn a reward that is meaningful to them (having more computer time, enjoying a special snack, having a guest lecturer or performer, spending class outside, etc.).

Completing Homework
Think Sheet

Name_____ Date_____

Write down any rooms or places inside your home (bedroom, kitchen, porch, living room, etc.) that have few distractions and give you enough space and resources to do homework:

-
-
-
-

What has kept you from completing a homework assignment on time, and how can you make sure that doesn't happen again?

What resources or materials should you always keep at your designated homework spot so you don't have to stop and search for them?

How does the skill of **Completing Homework** help you at school?

How does the skill of **Completing Homework** help you outside of school?

Completing Homework

1. Find out at school what the day's homework is for each subject.

2. Remember to bring home necessary books or materials in order to complete your assignments.

3. Get started on homework promptly, or at the designated time.

4. Complete all assignments accurately and neatly.

5. Carefully store completed homework until the next school day.

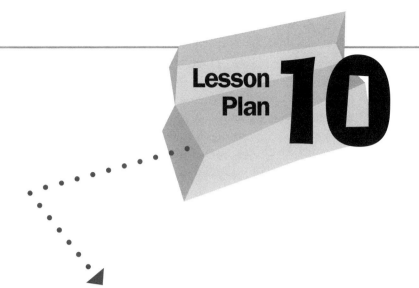

Making a Request (Asking a Favor)

Teacher Notes

Some students are notorious for demanding immediate help, expecting to always be first or telling (not asking) others what they want. By teaching students how to politely make a request or ask a favor, you can reduce the tension and hurt feelings that result when someone is verbally aggressive or overly demanding. In addition, the social climate of your learning community will improve.

Proactive Teaching Interaction

Introduce the Skill

Have students brainstorm reasons why it is important to know how to make a request or ask a favor. Reasons can include:

■ Shows respect

■ Helps you get what you want

■ Encourages others to say "Yes" to your request

Describe the Appropriate Behavior or Skill Steps

Making a Request (Asking a Favor)

1. **Look at the person.**

   ▪ Maintain eye contact.

2. **Use a clear, pleasant voice tone.**

   ▪ Don't mumble or shout.

3. **Make your request in the form of a question by saying "Would you…" and "Please…."**

   ▪ Don't assume you will get a "Yes" answer, and do not demand one.

4. **If your request is granted, remember to say "Thank you."**

5. **If your request is denied, remember to accept "No" for an answer.**

   ▪ Don't whine or pout.

Give a Reason or Rationale

Every day, we need to ask others for permission to do things or have things. Usually, when we ask someone for something, it is because we really want or need it. By following the behavioral steps of this skill, you can improve your chances of getting the answer or help you want. Other benefits of knowing how to make a request include:

■ Your calm and respectful behavior shows maturity and reason, which makes you look deserving of a "Yes" response.

■ Being respectful when you make a request or ask others for a favor makes them more open to sharing with you.

■ If you demand that others give you things or help you, they can become defensive and be unwilling to give you the answer or help you need.

Suggested Activities

Language Arts: Write the following quote from Mark Twain on the board or overhead. Have students read the quote and then write a short explanation that answers this question: Why does Twain consider a compliment worthless when it is accompanied by a request for a favor?

"Do not offer a compliment and ask a **favor** at the same time. A compliment that is charged for is not valuable."

Science/Math: Prior to sending students to the lab to conduct experiments, tell them there will be a limited number of supplies available (hide or lock away enough equipment so students will have to share). When lab groups need equipment that is being used by another group, they will have to make an appropriate request before gaining access to it. If a group takes materials without asking or makes an inappropriate request, have its members forfeit all of their supplies and start again.

Geography: Divide students into groups and instruct each group to create a poster depicting one of the continents. Give each group different resources and supplies they will have to share. For example, one group can use the Internet as a resource, a second group can have a geography book and a third group can have an atlas. Other groups won't have any resources that provide information about rivers, landmasses, etc., but they will have supplies, such as markers, scissors, glue, color pencils, etc., to create their posters. Groups will have to make appropriate requests to gain access to the materials they need.

Making a Request (Asking a Favor)
Suggested Role-Plays

Teacher Note:
Have students select one of the following scenarios to role-play in class.

1. You want to stay at a friend's house this weekend. Show how you would ask your parents for permission and include how you would accept both "Yes" and "No" answers.

2. You need a hall pass to leave the classroom and work in the media room. Show how you would ask the teacher for a hall pass.

3. You need to phone your mother, who is at work. Ask your teacher for permission to use the telephone in the principal's office.

4. You are told to work with two other students on a group project. After starting the project, you find out they want you to do most of the work. Ask permission from your teacher to be placed in a different group. Show how to accept both "Yes" and "No" answers.

5. Politely ask for a lunch ticket from the cafeteria manager.

6. You need to move all of the athletic equipment from the practice field into the gymnasium. Show or describe how you would ask your classmates to help you.

Making a Request
(Asking a Favor)
Think Sheet

Name_____ Date_____

List some times when you have had to make a request or ask a favor:

-

-

-

-

Why is it important to know how to properly make a request or ask someone for a favor?

When making a request, what voice tone (angry, sad, happy, quiet, etc.) should you use? Explain.

If your request is denied, how should you respond or react?

How can the skill of **Making a Request (Asking a Favor)** help you at school?

How can the skill of **Making a Request (Asking a Favor)** help you at home?

How can the skill of **Making a Request (Asking a Favor)** help you with friends?

Making a Request (Asking a Favor)

1. Look at the person.

2. Use a clear, pleasant voice tone.

3. Make your request in the form of a question by saying "Would you..." and "Please...."

4. If your request is granted, remember to say "Thank you."

5. If your request is denied, remember to accept "No" for an answer.

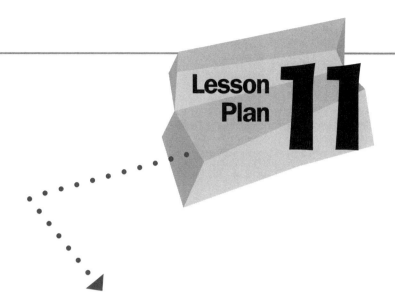

Accepting "No" for an Answer

Teacher Notes

There are two specific reasons why the skill of "Accepting 'No' for an Answer" can be especially difficult for students to learn. First, a student is oftentimes asking for something that he or she genuinely wants, so there can be real disappointment, frustration or even anger when the request is denied.

Second, the use of this skill involves *accepting* a "No" answer as the *final* answer. Many young people have learned that if they argue, whine, pout or complain loud enough or long enough, a "No" can turn into a "Yes." As a result, some students use inappropriate behaviors until they get the answer they want, and that reinforces their use of poor behaviors. All of this negative behavior creates a disruptive and chaotic environment. Therefore, it's critically important that you teach and practice the skill of "Accepting 'No' for an Answer" with students, reinforce them whenever they use the skill and calmly correct them whenever they act out inappropriately because they were told "No."

Proactive Teaching Interaction

Introduce the Skill

Have students brainstorm reasons why they should, or may have to, accept a "No" answer. Reasons can include:

- Saves time because you are not arguing or complaining
- Makes it more likely you will get a "Yes" answer in the future

■ Violates a class rule or school policy

■ Fosters a positive environment

■ Makes classroom activities run smoothly

Describe the Appropriate Behavior or Skill Steps

Accepting "No" for an Answer

1. **Look at the person.**

   ▪ Eye contact shows respect and says you're paying attention.

   ▪ Don't "stare down" or glare at the person.

   ▪ Maintain a pleasant or neutral facial expression; avoid frowning or making faces.

2. **Say "Okay," or nod to show understanding.**

   ▪ Saying "Okay" or nodding "Yes" communicates understanding, even though you may not agree with the answer.

   ▪ Answer right away and speak clearly; avoid using a harsh voice tone, arguing, whining or pouting.

   ▪ Nonverbal cues that show understanding include a "thumbs up" or an "Okay" hand sign.

3. **Stay calm.**

   ▪ If you react negatively, you may make the situation worse.

   ▪ To maintain self-control, use a calming-down strategy (deep breathing, counting to ten, taking a time-out, etc.).

4. **If you disagree, ask later.**

   ▪ Plan how you are going to approach the person who told you "No," including what you will say.

   ▪ Accept his or her answer, even if it is still "No."

   ▪ Thank the person for listening.

Give a Reason or Rationale

Being able to accept "No" answers shows maturity and demonstrates to others that you understand you won't always get what you want. Teachers, classmates and friends will appreciate and respect you more when you are cooperative and understanding. Knowing how to accept "No" has many other benefits:

■ You are more likely to get a "Yes" answer the next time you ask for something.

■ Others will appreciate your calm behavior and be respectful toward you.

■ Adults and peers will see you as someone who is mature, and they may be more willing to give you a "Yes" answer in situations that require more responsibility or leadership.

■ You make life easier and less stressful for everyone around you, and your relationships with others become more positive.

Suggested Activities

Language Arts: Have students write about a time when they did not accept "No" for an answer and what consequences, if any, followed. Ask for volunteers to share their stories aloud, and then discuss what lessons can be learned from their experiences.

Science/Math: In research studies, it's common practice to use surveys as a means of collecting data from individuals. Ask students to describe how they would approach someone to ask if he or she would complete a survey (allows you to review with students the skill of "Making a Request [Asking a Favor]"). Have students create a plan or strategy for responding to "No" answers, and then discuss their plans. Discussion topics can include how a small sample size (if too many people say "No") can skew a study's findings and other options for collecting data.

You also can have students use a daily or weekly calendar to track how often they are told "No" for a given period of time. Have students write notes on their calendars describing the circumstances surrounding each "No" answer, including their reaction. At the end of the day, week or month, have students tally the total number of "No" answers they recorded on their calendars and discuss. Discussion topics can include what day(s) had the most "No" answers and the possible reasons why, or how many times they reacted appropriately compared to how many times they did not accept "No."

Accepting "No" for an Answer
Suggested Role-Plays

Teacher Note:

Have students select one of the following scenarios to role-play in class.

1. You asked your parents if you could go to the movies with a friend. They said no. Accept their answer by following the four steps of the skill, and then politely ask for a reason why you are not allowed to go.

2. You asked your teacher if you could go to the library to check out a new book. Her answer was no. Show how to accept the answer using only nonverbal responses.

3. You were told to work on a group project with four other students, but you want to work with a different group. You asked the teacher if you could trade places with another student, and he said no. Describe behaviors or reactions you should avoid, and then show how to accept "No" appropriately.

4. At recess, you asked your friend to switch places with you so you could play goalie. Your friend said no. Show how you would accept a "No" answer from your friend.

Accepting "No" for an Answer
Think Sheet

Name_____ Date_____

Why is it sometimes hard to hear or accept a "No" answer?

List some times when you were told "No" by a parent, friend, teacher or principal:

-
-
-
-

List reasons why it's important to be able to accept "No" answers:

-

-

-

-

How can the skill of **Accepting "No" for an Answer** help you in the classroom?

How can the skill of **Accepting "No" for an Answer** help you on the playground or in athletics?

How can the skill of **Accepting "No" for an Answer** help you at home?

Accepting "No" for an Answer

1. **Look at the person.**

2. **Say "Okay," or nod to show understanding.**

3. **Stay calm.**

4. **If you disagree, ask later.**

Accepting Criticism or a Consequence

Teacher Notes

When introducing this lesson, we suggest you "disarm" the word "criticism" for students, especially if they associate the term with harsh or punishing statements. Brainstorm with students other words that can mean the same thing as criticism but sound less threatening. Examples include:

- Feedback
- Suggestions
- Advice
- Coaching
- Help

As you describe the skill's specific behavioral steps, remember to model the nonverbal behaviors, or "paraskills" (eye contact, voice tone and body language), you want to see from students. At Step 3 (stay calm), for example, you may want to have students role-play or describe behaviors associated with someone who is calm and under control. Also, you should discuss and practice various self-control strategies with students.

Proactive Teaching Interaction

Introduce the Skill

Brainstorm reasons why it is important to know how to accept criticism or a consequence. Reasons can include:

■ Creates a more positive environment

■ Enhances class morale when everyone is respectful

■ Increases the chances that future behaviors or actions will improve

■ Invites teachers and/or parents to work with you in positive and calm ways

■ Keeps you from repeating the same mistakes or errors

Describe the Appropriate Behavior or Skill Steps

Accepting Criticism or a Consequence

1. **Look at the person.**

   ▪ Remember that eye contact shows respect and helps focus your attention on the person.

2. **Say "Okay."**

   ▪ By saying "Okay," you communicate understanding. It doesn't necessarily mean, however, that you agree.

3. **Stay calm.**

   ▪ Your body language, including arms at your side, relaxed posture, neutral or pleasant facial expressions and a gentle voice tone, can help you communicate calmness.

   ▪ Use a self-control strategy (taking deep breaths, counting to ten, using positive self-talk, journaling, reminding yourself of the negative consequences if you argue, etc.) that will keep you from becoming overly emotional, angry or frustrated.

Give a Reason or Rationale

We all make mistakes and have to deal with negative feedback and criticism from time to time. Accepting criticism from teachers, bosses, friends and parents can help you avoid repeating mistakes or dealing with the same problems over and over again. Knowing how to accept criticism or a consequence has many benefits:

■ You can find out what you're doing wrong and work to correct it.

■ It can help you maintain relationships. If you argue when someone gives you constructive criticism, he or she may be less likely to help you or work with you in the future.

■ You show a willingness to change and improve.

■ Others may be more likely to praise you when you do a good job.

■ You can improve your relationships with authority figures because they will see you as someone who is mature and deserving of more opportunities or privileges.

■ You can prevent small issues from turning into significant problems.

Suggested Activities

Language Arts: Have students read Will Hobbs' *Downriver* (grades 7-12), Sid Fleischman's *The Whipping Boy* (grades 3-6) or any age-appropriate novel with a plot about taking ownership of one's behavior and dealing with the consequences of one's actions. Have students discuss how the lessons learned by the characters in the novel can apply to their own lives.

Physical Education: Use media stories about student-athletes caught hazing, using steroids or engaging in illegal activities to start a discussion about consequences. Use the stories as case studies to debate the appropriateness of the consequences and how well the individuals involved dealt with the fallout of their actions. Also talk about other consequences not mentioned in the stories or ones students may not have considered, such as the humiliation felt by hazing victims, the damage to a school's reputation and the emotional toll on family and friends. Review with students your school's expectations about fair play and respect.

History: Write the following quote from Corazon Aquino, the first female president of the Philippines, on the board or overhead.

"National leaders who find themselves wilting under the withering criticisms by members of the media, would do well not to take such criticism personally but to regard the media as their allies in keeping the government clean and honest, its services efficient and timely, and its commitment to democracy strong and unwavering."

Use the quote to start a discussion about how modern political leaders respond to criticism, both personal and professional, in a 24-hour media environment populated by political pundits and opinion makers. Ask students to consider how well they would handle public criticism, and if they agree with Aquino's comment. Have students research examples of political leaders (local, national or international) who changed their positions because of intense criticism or stood firm despite the public outcry.

Accepting Criticism or a Consequence
Suggested Role-Plays

Teacher Note:

Have students select one of the following scenarios to role-play in class.

1. Your teacher calls you to his desk to talk about the assignment you turned in. He tells you that your handwriting is so poor, he cannot read what you wrote. He also tells you that you skipped one of the questions. Show how to accept his criticisms by following the steps of the skill.

2. You shout at a friend who is walking in the hallway. A teacher stops you and tells you to lower your voice. Look at the teacher, say "Okay" and stay calm.

3. After making your bed, your mom walks in and says the covers are too wrinkled and the sides are uneven. Show or describe how you would accept her criticisms.

4. Your parents ask you to clean the garage while they go to the store. Instead, you watch television. When they come home and see you have not done anything, they take away your allowance for a week. Following the steps of the skill, show how you would accept the consequence.

5. During a basketball game, you turn the ball over on back-to-back possessions. After the second turnover, your coach calls a timeout and screams at you to get your head in the game. Show how you would accept his criticism appropriately.

6. You have a new job at a fast food restaurant where several of your friends work. One evening, your boss catches you goofing off and making inappropriate comments to co-workers. Your boss ushers you into the office, tells you that your behavior is unprofessional and sends you home early. Describe how you would accept the criticism and the consequence appropriately.

Accepting Criticism
or a Consequence
Think Sheet

Name_____ Date_____

List other words that mean the same thing as "criticism":

What are some reasons why you should learn how to accept criticism or a consequence?

-
-
-
-

During the school day, when or where is it hardest for you to accept criticism? Explain.

What can you say or do to keep your cool when you get criticism from a teacher or parent?

How can the skill of **Accepting Criticism or a Consequence** help you at school?

How can the skill of **Accepting Criticism or a Consequence** help you at home?

Accepting Criticism or a Consequence

1. Look at the person.

2. Say "Okay."

3. Stay calm.

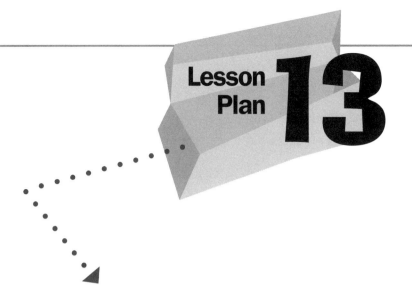

Disagreeing Appropriately

Teacher Notes

"Disagreeing Appropriately" is a skill that empowers students with the ability to stand up for themselves in a way that is respectful and dignified. As students reach adolescence, this skill is essential because developmentally "normal" disagreements become more common between students and their teachers, parents and peers.

When you teach this lesson, some ancillary instruction about *when* and *where* to disagree is helpful, especially as it relates to the classroom. In addition, a logical progression or link from this lesson can be made to the skill of "Accepting Decisions of Authority." Students need to be reminded that disagreeing with someone, even when done in a mature and appropriate manner, does not guarantee that the other person will change his or her opinion or decision.

Proactive Teaching Interaction

Introduce the Skill

Start your discussion by using a video clip from a movie, television show or news program that depicts a disagreement – a coach arguing with an official, a lawyer arguing with a judge or friends arguing with each other. Have students reflect on the behaviors they saw and the language they heard, and then ask them to write a brief summary describing a situation where they had a disagreement at school or home.

As a class, discuss these experiences and then brainstorm reasons why it's important to know how to disagree appropriately. Reasons can include:

■ Avoids shouting matches and hurt feelings

■ Helps you remain calm and respectful

■ Makes it more likely that opinions will be taken more seriously

■ Shows maturity

Describe the Appropriate Behavior or Skill Steps

Disagreeing Appropriately

1. **Look at the person.**

   ▪ Again, you do not want to "stare down" or glare at the person you're arguing with.

2. **Use a pleasant voice tone.**

3. **Say "I understand how you feel."**

   ▪ An empathy statement communicates your willingness to try to understand and respect the person's point of view.

4. **Tell why you feel differently.**

   ▪ Explain your point of view.

5. **Give a reason.**

   ▪ Use facts or experiences to support your viewpoint.

6. **Listen to the other person.**

   ▪ The more respect you show, the more respect you will receive.

   ▪ Be willing to "agree to disagree."

Give a Reason or Rationale

By learning how to disagree appropriately, you can avoid angry arguments and unpleasant situations that can arise when others do not share your opinion. Knowing how to explain your feelings or attitudes in a calm and respectful manner creates a positive environment where everyone feels comfortable to express their thoughts. Other benefits of knowing how to disagree appropriately include:

■ Your opinion may be taken more seriously if you can clearly explain your position and offer supporting reasons.

■ Others will be able to understand your position, and the issue or problem may get resolved more quickly without hurting anyone's feelings.

■ When you show respect to whomever you disagree with – teacher, coach, friend, sibling, parent, etc. – he or she will be more willing to listen to you.

■ Others will see you as someone who is reasonable, mature and thoughtful.

Suggested Activities

Language Arts: Have students think about disagreements they have had with others and write a fictional conversation that incorporates skill Steps 3, 4 and 5. Older students, for example, can create a conversation they would have with a boss who scheduled them to work every weekend for a month. Younger students can create a conversation they would have with a teacher who did not give them full credit on an essay question. Have students read their conversations aloud and, as a group, discuss how well their conversations reflect the skill.

Government: Use the history of the Olympic Games to showcase how nations, athletes and others express disagreement in real and symbolic ways. Examples to cite include the 1968 Mexico City Olympics and the "Black Power" salute, the 1972 Olympics and the assassination of Israeli athletes and the 1980 and 1984 boycotts. Have students research the motivations behind the salute, assassinations and boycotts, and then discuss whether or not the Olympics are an appropriate venue for expressing political and social grievances.

Science/Math: Relate the experiences of Galileo and Copernicus to the skill of "Disagreeing Appropriately." Explain to students that mathematicians and scientists like Galileo and Copernicus were instrumental in developing new ideas and solving many of the "mysteries" of the universe. However, prior to their discoveries and those of others, the ideas of Aristotle were considered scientific fact. Not only were Aristotle's ideas accepted as fact, the church treated his theories as laws. Those who disagreed with these laws were called heretics and persecuted for their beliefs. Copernicus and Galileo were jailed and others were harmed because their views contradicted the teachings of Aristotle and the "laws" of the church. Many people who read their writings disagreed with Copernicus and Galileo simply because they contradicted the beliefs of the church, not because they disagreed with the science or reasoning behind their theories and ideas.

Have students reflect on the experiences of Galileo and Copernicus and then discuss how people living in that time could have disagreed in more appropriate ways. You also can discuss how disagreements can lead to better science and scientific truth.

History/Social Studies: When discussing or teaching the American Revolution, have students read James Lincoln Collier's *My Brother Sam Is Dead*. Use the war and the fictional tale of the Meeker family to highlight how people respond to conflict and the potential it has to tear them apart. Have students create scenarios where the colonists and the British resolve their differences without resorting to war, and then discuss how realistic or plausible those alternative scenarios are.

Disagreeing Appropriately
Suggested Role-Plays

Teacher Note:
Have students select one of the following scenarios to role-play in class.

1. Your basketball team loses the game because of a last-second foul. You think the referees were unfair and favored the other team. Show how you would respectfully disagree with the referee's call.

2. You earned second place in the school's essay contest, but you think the winner cheated on his essay. Show or describe how you would disagree with the results.

3. The teacher hands back yesterday's quiz. Your answers to questions 3 and 4 are marked as incorrect. Your neighbor, who had the same answers as you for those questions, has his answers marked correct. Describe how you would approach the teacher and dispute your grade.

4. Your parents won't let you see any of your friends over the weekend because you didn't finish your chores. You think the punishment is too harsh. Show how to appropriately disagree with their decision.

5. Your parents want you to go to bed at the same time as your brother (or sister), who is two years younger than you. Show how you would tell them you think you should be allowed to stay up later.

Disagreeing Appropriately
Think Sheet

Name_____ Date _____

Why is it important for you to know how to disagree with others in an appropriate way?

Who is the person (teacher, sibling, parent, friend, etc.) you have the most disagreements with, and is it difficult for you to disagree appropriately with him or her? Explain.

What words or actions can you say or do to keep a disagreement from turning into a shouting match or fight?

Part of disagreeing appropriately involves using an empathy statement. What are some examples of empathy statements you can say during a disagreement?

-

-

-

How can the skill of **Disagreeing Appropriately** help you at school?

How can the skill of **Disagreeing Appropriately** help you at home?

Disagreeing Appropriately

1. Look at the person.

2. Use a pleasant voice tone.

3. Say "I understand how you feel."

4. Tell why you feel differently.

5. Give a reason.

6. Listen to the other person.

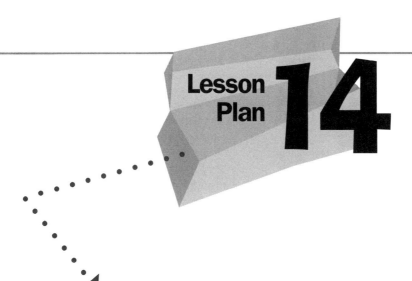

Advocating for Oneself

Teacher Notes

This is an important life skill that teaches students how to stand up for themselves when they are being treated unfairly or taken advantage of, or having their problems ignored.

Educators are often tempted to emphasize this skill when responding to bullying problems. However, it is important to note that bullying typically is characterized by an imbalance of power (physical or social) between the bully and the victim. The skill of "Advocating for Oneself" is more effective and appropriate in situations where power imbalances are not an issue and there is no history of repeated physical, sexual or emotional abuse. For insights into how to deal with bullying and the social skills that can help bullies, victims and bystanders, we recommend reading *No Room for Bullies: From the Classroom to Cyberspace* (a Boys Town Press publication edited by José Bolton and Stan Graeve).

Proactive Teaching Interaction

Introduce the Skill

Have students brainstorm reasons why it is important to know how to advocate for themselves. Reasons can include:

- Builds self-confidence
- Prevents others from taking advantage of you
- Shows maturity
- Helps establish boundaries   physical and emotional

Describe the Appropriate Behavior or Skill Steps

Advocating for Oneself

1. **Identify a situation in which you should advocate for yourself.**

   - Appropriate situations include when you are being teased or treated unfairly.

2. **Remember to remain calm and use a pleasant or neutral voice tone.**

   - Avoid yelling or saying things that are hurtful to someone else.

3. **Describe your point of view or the outcome you desire.**

   - Avoid vague comments or sounding hesitant; be specific and assertive.

4. **Give rationales for advocating for yourself.**

   - Reasons might include unfair treatment, poor service or trying to prevent arguments and fights.

5. **Thank the person for listening.**

Give a Reason or Rationale

As you grow older, you won't always have a teacher, parent or friend who will be there to stick up for you or defend you. Knowing how to advocate for yourself can give you the confidence to handle difficult situations or people on your own. Other benefits of knowing how to advocate on your own behalf include:

- You show others that you're not a pushover.

- You don't allow others to take advantage of you.

- You develop confidence and are more likely to advocate for others, too.

- Others will see that you know how to be responsible and handle problems.

Suggested Activities

Language Arts: Have students write a short paragraph describing in detail a situation where they will need to advocate for themselves (talking to a coach about getting more playing time, asking an employer for time off, asking a teacher for a deadline extension, etc.). When they've written their paragraphs, have students work in pairs or small groups. Each group member should read his or her situation aloud and ask for advice on how best to advocate for what he or she wants. After a group discussion, students should write out the steps and words they will use when the situation arises.

History: Have students research an individual who was an effective advocate for change at the local, state or national level. The individual's advocacy can relate to human rights, medical research or funding, new legislation, environmental issues, animal rights, peace, etc. Ask students to identify the characteristics of the individual that made him or her an effective agent for change.

Advocating for Oneself
Suggested Role-Plays

Teacher Note:
Have students select one of the following scenarios to role-play in class.

1. You think your math teacher does not give you as much help or attention as others in the class. Following the steps of the skill, show what you would do to receive more time from the teacher.

2. In the cafeteria, students sitting at another table keep tossing pieces of food at you and your friends. You try ignoring the behavior, hoping it will stop, but they continue to throw food. Show how you would step up to end the childish behavior by calmly, but firmly, advocating on behalf of everyone at your table.

3. You're playing with your dog in a neighborhood park when a stranger tells you that dogs don't belong there. The stranger tells you to leave. However, there are other dogs in the park, and you know there is no rule against having dogs in the park. Show how you would stand up for your right to be in the park with your dog.

4. Your parents are going out for the evening and plan to hire a baby sitter. You think you are responsible enough to stay home alone. Describe how you would convince your parents that you do not need a baby sitter.

Advocating for Oneself
Think Sheet

Name_____ Date _____

What does the word "advocate" mean to you?

Why is it important to know how to advocate for yourself?

List some times when you will need to advocate for yourself rather than depend on others:

- ▪
- ▪
- ▪
- ▪

How can using the skill of **Advocating for Oneself** help you in the classroom?

How can using the skill of **Advocating for Oneself** help you outside of school?

Advocating for Oneself

1. **Identify a situation in which you should advocate for yourself.**

2. **Remember to remain calm and use a pleasant or neutral voice tone.**

3. **Describe your point of view or the outcome you desire.**

4. **Give rationales for advocating for yourself.**

5. **Thank the person for listening.**

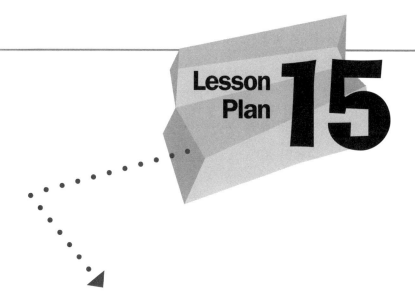

Making an Appropriate Complaint

Teacher Notes

Too often, students express their displeasure about a situation by complaining loudly, whining, blaming others or making personal attacks. By helping students learn how to make a complaint in an appropriate manner, you can give them a stronger voice when they feel victimized or want their concerns known. This skill will not only empower students, but also help you reduce some of the drama that disrupts your learning environment.

Proactive Teaching Interaction

Introduce the Skill

Start a discussion by asking students to describe what they said or did when they made a complaint at school or home. Have students identify situations where they think it is appropriate to complain, and then brainstorm reasons why it is important to know how to make an appropriate complaint. Reasons can include:

- Demonstrates respect and shows maturity
- Makes it easier to achieve a resolution
- Helps others recognize a mistake or misunderstanding
- Prevents hurt feelings
- Creates a more positive environment at school

Describe the Appropriate Behavior or Skill Steps

Making an Appropriate Complaint

1. **Look at the person.**
   - Eye contact helps communicate the seriousness and sincerity of your complaint.

2. **Phrase your complaint as an objective problem, not a personal attack.**
   - Avoid accusations, such as "You're not being fair!" Instead, say something like, "This situation is unfair."

3. **Remain calm and pleasant.**
   - Do not scream, use threatening gestures or stare down the other person.

4. **Be assertive, but avoid repeating your complaint over and over.**
   - Be prepared to accept a "No" answer.

5. **Thank the person for his or her cooperation.**
   - Be courteous, even if your complaint is not corrected to your satisfaction.

Give a Reason or Rationale

When most people make a complaint, they want to be heard and have their concerns taken seriously. Unfortunately, complaints sometimes are expressed in angry or threatening ways that make others less willing to listen or help. Knowing how to make an appropriate complaint can prevent disagreements from becoming shouting matches, and help you reach a resolution sooner. Other benefits of knowing how to make an appropriate complaint include:

- You can make others aware of a problem or issue that they did not know existed.

- You can prevent a problem or mistake from happening again.

- Others will take you seriously and won't dismiss you as a whiner or "chronic complainer."

- Sharing your feelings can make you feel better, even if nothing can be done.

Suggested Activities

Language Arts: Do a creative exercise in which students write a story or play around the theme of making a complaint. Plot lines can include the negative consequences of not using the skill or the positive outcomes that result from using the skill. Or, they can write about someone who complains too much or too little and the problems that result. Have students act out their stories or plays and then discuss what lessons can be learned.

Government: Have students research the steps for filing various types of complaints with local, state or federal agencies. Ask students to explain in an essay or oral report why filing a formal complaint can be beneficial even when an individual's complaint cannot be resolved to his or her satisfaction.

Making an Appropriate Complaint
Suggested Role-Plays

Teacher Note:

Have students select one of the following scenarios to role-play in class.

1. At recess, everyone always plays soccer, but you want to play basketball. You don't think it's fair that soccer is the only recess game you get to play. Following the steps of the skill, show how you would complain to your friends and the teacher.

2. Your teacher gave you a "B" for your essay about mountain lions. You think your essay deserved an "A." Show how you would approach the teacher to complain about your grade.

3. At home, it's your job to do the dishes after dinner. Your brother's job is to take the family dog for a walk. You don't think it's fair that you always get stuck doing the dishes. Describe how you would make an appropriate complaint to your parents.

4. You think your teacher gives more attention to other students and always calls on them, even though you raise your hand to answer questions, too. Show how you would complain about this situation and include the best time(s) to approach the teacher (during class, before class, after school, etc.).

5. Last weekend, your parents told your sister to clean out the garage. She did, but she forgot to clean and organize the shelves. Your parents tell you to finish cleaning the garage this weekend, but you think your sister should do it. Describe how you would make an appropriate complaint to your parents, and then describe how you would complain to your sister in a calm, polite way.

Making an Appropriate Complaint
Think Sheet

Name_____ Date_____

Why should you learn how to make a complaint in a polite or calm way?

One step in the skill of **Making an Appropriate Complaint** involves focusing on the problem rather than the person. What can you say to someone that will help keep the conversation or complaint focused on solving a problem instead of blaming a person?

-

-

-

-

How can using the skill of **Making an Appropriate Complaint** help you at school?

How can using the skill of **Making an Appropriate Complaint** improve the relationships you have with your parents or siblings?

Making an Appropriate Complaint

1. Look at the person.

2. Phrase your complaint as an objective problem, not a personal attack.

3. Remain calm and pleasant.

4. Be assertive, but avoid repeating your complaint over and over.

5. Thank the person for his or her cooperation.

Choosing Appropriate Words to Say

Teacher Notes

Most students use words and phrases in the classroom that they hear at home, in their neighborhoods and from the music and entertainment programs that populate the airwaves. Unfortunately, some of their lingo is crude, crass and contrary to the behavioral expectations you have for your learning community. In addition, some students have a habit of blurting out comments that are insensitive or wholly inappropriate for the situation or environment. By teaching students how to be more thoughtful and selective about the words they use and what they say, you can foster an environment that is more welcoming, respectful and polite.

Proactive Teaching Interaction

Introduce the Skill

Visit an online Web site, such as washingtonpost.com or nytimes.com, and show students the site's discussion policy that explains the restrictions for posting comments on its discussion boards. Ask students what they think the purpose of such a policy is and if a similar policy about language use in the classroom should be adopted at your school.

After the discussion, have students brainstorm reasons why knowing how to choose appropriate words is important. Reasons can include:

■ Makes it less likely others will be offended or hurt

■ Shows respect for others

- Sets a good example for others
- Improves the social climate of the classroom or school

Describe the Appropriate Behavior or Skill Steps

Choosing Appropriate Words to Say

1. **Look at the situation and the people around you.**

2. **Know the meanings of words you are about to say.**
   - If you do not know what a word means, avoid saying the word.

3. **Refrain from using words that will offend people around you or that they will not understand.**
   - If you are around people you do not know very well, use words or make comments that would be appropriate to say in front of a grandparent, employer or religious figure.
   - Avoid using a foreign language around people who do not know the language.
   - Avoid using street lingo in formal settings, such as school, work and public businesses.

4. **Avoid using slang, profanity or words that could have a sexual meaning.**

5. **Decide what thoughts you want to put into words and then say the words.**

Give a Reason or Rationale

Everyone experiences moments when they wish they could take back something they said. A misstatement, glib remark or four-letter word uttered at the wrong time and heard by the wrong person can be a source of shame and embarrassment for the speaker and listener. By learning how to choose appropriate words and understanding what's acceptable in different social settings, you can reduce verbal blunders. Other benefits of knowing how to choose appropriate words include:

- You are less likely to be misunderstood.
- You can expand your vocabulary.
- You show good manners and intelligence.
- You can avoid insensitive comments.
- Others will perceive you as mature and socially skilled.
- You are more likely to earn leadership roles and be given more opportunities.

Suggested Activities

Language Arts: Write the poem *The Rainy Day* by Henry Wadsworth Longfellow on the board or overhead. Read the poem aloud and then ask students to think about his word choices, including the poem's title. Lead a group discussion about the words, word patterns and metaphors that Longfellow used. Ask students to define the "mood" or "rhythm" of the poem and explain how his words evoke that "mood." Have students think of other possible titles that communicate or capture the meaning of his poem and discuss them.

The Rainy Day

The day is cold, and dark, and dreary;

It rains, and the wind is never weary;

The vine still clings to the mouldering wall,

But at every gust more dead leaves fall,

And the day is dark and dreary.

My life is cold and dark and dreary;

It rains and the wind is never weary;

My thoughts still cling to the mouldering past,

And youth's fond hopes fall thick in the blast,

And my life is dark and dreary.

Be still, sad heart and cease repining;

Behind the clouds is the sun still shining;

Thy fate is the common fate of all,

Into each life some rain must fall,

Some days must be dark and dreary.

History/Government: Have students read and critique the words, phrases and themes of any presidential inaugural address. Discuss different aspects of the speech, including how the president's words reflected the times in which he governed and what phrases or lines were inspirational to the American people.

Science/Math: Select a study from any peer-reviewed scientific journal and give copies to each student. Read selective portions of the study and point out instances where the authors had to use precise language to describe the study's methodology and why, when summarizing the results, phrases such as "suggests" or "indicates" are used instead of "proves" or "disproves." Discuss how a researcher's word choices must accurately reflect the findings of his or her study.

Choosing Appropriate Words to Say
Suggested Role-Plays

Teacher Note:

Have students select one of the following scenarios to role-play in class.

1. You and a friend are walking to your next class and talking about what you did over the weekend. Following the steps of the skill, have an appropriate conversation.

2. In class, a student you do not know very well asks if you get your clothes from the local dump. You are not sure if he's being mean and rude, making a joke or just trying to strike up a conversation. Describe how you would respond to his remark.

3. The principal's spouse recently passed away, and you want to express your sympathy the next time you see her at school. Describe what you would say to the principal.

4. You see your favorite teacher at an outdoor musical concert. Greet him and start a conversation about the show.

Choosing Appropriate Words to Say

Think Sheet

Name_____ Date_____

List some times or situations where it is helpful to know how to choose the right words:

- ■

- ■

- ■

- ■

Why is it helpful to think about what you want to say before you start talking?

What words are appropriate to say to a friend whose pet is missing?

What words are appropriate to say to a classmate who has a serious illness?

Where or in what situations is it appropriate to use slang words? Where or in what situations is the use of slang disrespectful?

How can the skill of **Choosing Appropriate Words to Say** help you at school?

How can the skill of **Choosing Appropriate Words to Say** help you outside of school?

Choosing Appropriate Words to Say

1. Look at the situation and the people around you.

2. Know the meanings of words you are about to say.

3. Refrain from using words that will offend people around you or that they will not understand.

4. Avoid using slang, profanity or words that could have a sexual meaning.

5. Decide what thoughts you want to put into words and then say the words.

son
lan **17**

Accepting Decisions of Authority

Teacher Notes

Many students, especially adolescents, will at some point challenge your decisions. However, if students regularly disregard your authority or refuse to accept your decisions and those of administrators, managing the classroom and dealing with disruptive behaviors becomes nearly impossible. Unfortunately, some students have learned that if they threaten, act out or carry on, they can reverse any decision or reduce any punishment. If you allow students to get away with manipulative behaviors that undermine your decisions, expect to see more argumentative and confrontational responses from them. This is especially true when you're correcting their misbehaviors and making discipline decisions.

As you help students learn this skill, assess your own approach to discipline. Are your discipline decisions consistent and fair, or are they arbitrary and rash? If students perceive them to be the latter, they have little incentive to follow your rules or engage in appropriate behaviors.

Proactive Teaching Interaction

Introduce the Skill

Have students brainstorm reasons why it is important for them to respect and accept the decisions of authority figures at school and in the community. Reasons can include:

■ Prevents you from getting into dangerous or troubling situations

■ Reduces chaos and keeps order

- Shows respect and demonstrates maturity
- Reinforces the social and behavioral expectations in your community
- Sets a good example for your peers and others

Describe the Appropriate Behavior or Skill Steps

Accepting Decisions of Authority

1. **Look at the person.**

   - Don't stare, make faces or roll your eyes.

2. **Remain calm and monitor your feelings and behavior.**

   - If you feel yourself getting emotional, take deep breaths, silently count to ten or use another strategy to calm yourself.

3. **Use a pleasant or neutral tone of voice.**

4. **Acknowledge the decision by saying "Okay" or "Yes, I understand."**

   - Don't argue; be respectful.
   - Keep the interaction cordial.
   - Avoid using harsh words or a hostile voice tone.

5. **If you disagree, do so at a later time.**

   - Ask the person if you can speak to him or her at a later time.
   - If the person does not want to talk with you, respect the decision.
   - If the person agrees to talk with you, have a plan for what you want to say that includes specific reasons why you disagree.

6. **Refrain from arguing, pouting or becoming angry.**

   - The decision may not change, so be prepared to accept a "No" answer.

Give a Reason or Rationale

By definition, authority figures have the experience, knowledge and power to make decisions that directly affect you. While you might not always agree with them, most authority figures have your best interests at heart. If you can look at the decisions from their perspective, you're more likely to understand their reasoning, learn from the decisions and make better choices for yourself in the future. Other benefits of knowing how to accept the decisions of authority figures include:

- You show your respect and, in turn, earn respect.

■ You avoid saying or doing anything that will create more tension or cause trouble.

■ You avoid earning negative consequences for arguing or being confrontational.

■ Others will see your maturity, and they may be more willing to include you in future decisions when appropriate.

Suggested Activities

Government/History: The United States Supreme Court has the final say on questions related to the Constitution and the laws of the United States. Select a prominent or controversial court decision that divided the public or caused passionate debate. Examples can include *Dred Scott v. Sanford, Roe v. Wade, Brown v. Board of Education* and *District of Columbia v. Heller.*

Discuss the public's response (protest marches, demonstrations, additional legal challenges, celebrations, etc.), and relate it back to the issue of accepting decisions of authority. Topics for discussion can include the time, energy and money that are sometimes invested in challenging authority. Also talk about the risks, including loss of reputation or freedom. Ask students to think about when it is appropriate to take risks and make sacrifices to challenge authority and when it is not. Also remind students that disagreeing appropriately does not guarantee a decision will be overturned.

Science/Math: Read the following paragraph aloud and ask students to answer questions about accepting decisions of authority. Questions can include:

- Did Einstein accept the decision of the government?

- Do you think he should have responded differently to the government's decision? Why or why not? Explain your position.

Albert Einstein is best known for his Theory of Relativity. However, he also was instrumental in the development of nuclear physics. The locations and workings of the parts of the atom were important developments in science and physics. That understanding opened many new research opportunities. The United States government was interested in applying the research to military weapons, such as atomic bombs. Einstein pleaded with members of the government to channel the knowledge about the atom toward more productive and peaceful pursuits. His concerns were noted but ignored as the government launched the Manhattan Project to build an atomic bomb.

Einstein chose not to assist the government in this effort, which he considered dangerous and destructive for humanity.

Accepting Decisions
of Authority
Suggested Role-Plays

Teacher Note:

Have students select one of the following scenarios to role-play in class.

1. Your team will play the state's top-ranked team on Saturday. Friends and family from out of town are coming to see you play. Two days before the game, your coach catches you goofing off during practice and suspends you from the team. You won't be able to play in the big game. You think the coach's decision is too harsh and that you deserve to play on Saturday. Using the steps of the skill, show how you would accept the decision but also let the coach know you disagree.

2. Your parents ground you for a week because you missed curfew by 30 minutes. You don't think you should be punished at all because car trouble caused you to be late. Show how you would disagree appropriately, but ultimately accept their decision.

3. You ask your parents if you can adopt a dog as a family pet. They say no because you are too young and not responsible enough. Describe how you could advocate for getting a pet while also accepting their decision.

4. Everyone in your history class scores poorly on a unit exam. On Friday, the teacher decides the class needs more instruction, so she gives you homework that includes reading several chapters from the textbook and writing a five-page essay. The assignment is due Monday. Describe reactions or behaviors that are inappropriate or show disrespect to the teacher, and then show how you would appropriately accept her decision.

Accepting Decisions of Authority
Think Sheet

Name_____ Date_____

Who are some of the authority figures in your life?

Pick two of the authority figures you identified above and describe why it is important for you to accept their decisions.

If you disagree with an authority figure's decision, what words or actions are okay to say or show?

How can the skill of **Accepting Decisions of Authority** help you at school?

How can the skill of **Accepting Decisions of Authority** help you in sports?

How can the skill of **Accepting Decisions of Authority** help you at home?

Accepting Decisions of Authority

1. Look at the person.

2. Remain calm and monitor your feelings and behavior.

3. Use a pleasant or neutral tone of voice.

4. Acknowledge the decision by saying "Okay" or "Yes, I understand."

5. If you disagree, do so at a later time.

6. Refrain from arguing, pouting or becoming angry.

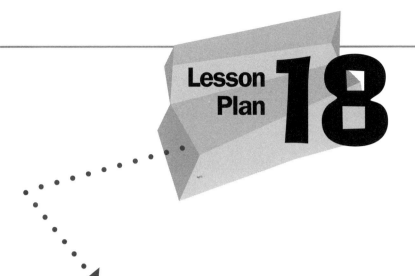

Using Anger-Control Strategies

Teacher Notes

Students who do not know how to calm down or manage their feelings of anger often have emotional meltdowns that involve name calling, screaming, cursing, tossing books and slamming desks. These inappropriate behavioral expressions often occur when students are being disciplined or corrected. For many, they simply don't know any other way to express how they feel. You can use this lesson to help students develop a "staying calm" plan so they have an individualized and practical way to manage their anger or frustration.

You also may need to remind students that anger itself is not "bad" or "wrong." Anger is a natural emotion that can be healthy, provided students express their feelings in ways that are constructive rather than destructive.

Proactive Teaching Interaction

Introduce the Skill

Ask students to describe what they feel (jumpy, hot, tightened muscles, etc.) as they get angry or start to lose emotional control. Continue the discussion by asking what, if anything, they do to try to calm themselves. Have students brainstorm strategies for managing their emotions. Strategies can include:

■ Deep breathing

■ Muscle relaxation

■ Positive self-talk

■ Counting to ten

■ Journaling

■ Taking a time-out

■ Visualization techniques

■ Physical exercise

Describe the Appropriate Behavior or Skill Steps

Using Anger-Control Strategies

1. **Learn what situations cause you to lose control or make you angry.**

2. **Monitor the feelings you have in stressful situations.**

   ▪ Pay attention to your body. Signs that you may be getting frustrated or angry include tense muscles, dry mouth, raised voice, pounding heart, sweaty palms and aggressive body movements.

3. **Instruct yourself to breathe deeply and relax when stressful feelings begin to arise.**

   ▪ Take a deep breath and exhale slowly; repeat if necessary.

4. **Reword angry feelings so they can be expressed appropriately and calmly to others.**

   ▪ You don't have to shout or scream to express disappointment or frustration.

   ▪ Instead of always trying to convince others you're right and they're wrong, accept the fact that sometimes you need to "agree to disagree."

   ▪ Reframe the situation and look at it from a different perspective; instead of focusing on the fact that you are mad, channel your anger into solving or correcting the situation.

5. **Praise yourself for controlling emotional outbursts.**

Give a Reason or Rationale

It is important to stay calm since worse things always seem to happen if you lose your temper. Using an anger-control strategy can calm your nerves and help clear your mind so you can make better choices and avoid even more problems. Other benefits of using anger-control strategies include:

■ You show others that you can keep your "cool" and are responsible.

- You earn others' respect because you show maturity and self-control.

- Others will see that you can handle bad situations, and they may rely on you more.

- You are much less likely to feel regret about your behavior.

- You avoid escalating situations, damaging relationships and hurting friendships.

Suggested Activities

Language Arts: Select a short story for students to read or have them read chapters from *The Scarlet Letter* (grades 9-12), *Animal Farm* (grades 7-12), *Lord of the Flies* (grades 8-12) or *Friends and Enemies* (grades 4-6) and discuss how certain characters expressed their anger. Ask students to identify other, more positive responses the characters could have had to their situations. Then have them rewrite a scene based on one of the appropriate responses.

Science: Test how well students can analyze their feelings. Have students record how they feel at a given moment (excited, nervous, sad, indifferent, etc.), and then have them test their self-analysis by putting on a mood ring. Discuss the scientific process behind how mood rings work and why they may not always be accurate.

History/Social Studies: Study the life and work of Mahatma Gandhi, and ask students to identify other prominent leaders who were inspired to follow his example of non-violence and peaceful resistance.

Using Anger-Control Strategies

Suggested Role-Plays

Teacher Note:

Have students select one of the following scenarios to role-play in class.

1. You find out that the class bully attacked one of your best friends during PE class. You are very upset and want to beat up the bully. Show how you would calm yourself before approaching the bully, and how you would confront the bully without using physical violence.

2. Your teacher warns you not to pass notes during class, and then you earn a detention from the teacher for talking in class. You are mad and feel the teacher is picking on you. Show how you would express your frustration to the teacher.

3. You just finished an art project that took you three weeks to complete. A classmate in the art room accidentally drops a can of pink paint, splattering you and your project. Your shirt is ruined and your art project has to be repaired. Show how you would control your anger and react calmly to the student who spilled the paint.

4. Your brother broke the iPod that your parents gave you for your birthday. He laughs, tosses it at you and says "Oops." Show how you would control your anger and deal with the situation.

Using Anger-Control Strategies
Think Sheet

Name_____ Date_____

What does self-control mean to you?

What makes you mad?

How can you tell when you are getting angry or starting to lose control?

Which of the following anger-control strategies do you think would be most helpful to you? Explain.

- Deep breathing and muscle relaxation

- Counting to ten

- Positive self-talk

- Journaling

- Taking a time-out (walking away or leaving a situation)

- Visualization (imagining a garden, forest or other peaceful scene)

- Other _____

How do you know when you have regained self-control?

How can the skill of **Using Anger-Control Strategies** help you in the classroom?

How can the skill of **Using Anger-Control Strategies** help you at home?

Using Anger-Control Strategies

1. Learn what situations cause you to lose control or make you angry.

2. Monitor the feelings you have in stressful situations.

3. Instruct yourself to breathe deeply and relax when stressful feelings begin to arise.

4. Reword angry feelings so they can be expressed appropriately and calmly to others.

5. Praise yourself for controlling emotional outbursts.

Making an Apology (Saying You're Sorry)

Teacher Notes

Acts of kindness can help students build healthier, more respectful relationships with each other. One act of kindness is admitting mistakes and saying "I'm sorry." Disagreements, accidents and misunderstandings do happen at school. If students never apologize, or seem insincere when they do, an environment of resentment and bitterness can easily develop. In such an unforgiving atmosphere, behavior problems and classroom disruptions can occur with greater frequency.

If administrators or behavior interventionists at your school use the Boys Town Administrative Intervention Model, then the skill of "Making an Apology" will be a component of the office referral process. One way students earn their way back into the classroom is through using this skill. By teaching students how to make an apology, you not only help them acquire a life-long skill, but also help to reinforce the behavior expectations and policies of your school.

Proactive Teaching Interaction

Introduce the Skill

Begin your discussion by demonstrating and distinguishing various types of apologies, such as how an apology to a friend or sibling might look and sound different from an apology made to a teacher or a friend's parent. Remind students that saying they're sorry sometimes won't be enough to correct a situation, and they will have to do more to rebuild trust, earn forgiveness and fix the problem.

Have students brainstorm reasons why it is important to know how to make an apology. Reasons can include:

■ Shows maturity

■ Helps repair relationships

■ Makes forgiveness more likely

■ Shows respect

Describe the Appropriate Behavior or Skill Steps

Making an Apology (Saying You're Sorry)

1. **Look at the person.**

   ▪ Eye contact shows respect for the person receiving the apology and helps communicate your sincerity.

   ▪ Have a pleasant or neutral facial expression; avoid frowning or laughing.

2. **Use a serious, sincere voice tone, but don't pout.**

   ▪ An appropriate voice tone communicates to the person that your apology is genuine.

   ▪ Avoid using a tone that sounds condescending, dismissive or phony.

3. **Begin by saying, "I wanted to apologize for..." or "I'm sorry for...."**

   ▪ Say specifically what you did that caused the pain, hurt or embarrassment.

4. **Do not make excuses or try to rationalize your behavior.**

   ▪ Own up to your actions.

5. **Sincerely say that you will try not to repeat the same behavior in the future.**

   ▪ Say what you will do in the future to avoid repeating the same mistake.

6. **Offer to compensate or pay restitution.**

   ▪ Sometimes saying you're sorry won't be enough, especially if property, such as books or clothes, are damaged or destroyed.

7. **Thank the other person for listening.**

Give a Reason or Rationale

Everyone makes errors in judgment or does something that hurts or disappoints others. When you can recognize such mistakes or realize when you have "goofed," you can try to correct the situation and soothe hurt feelings. Making an apology is the first step. It may not always make everything okay, but it starts the healing process. Other benefits of knowing how to make an apology include:

■ Apologizing is a necessary skill for maintaining friendships.

■ An apology shows that you recognize your mistakes and are mature enough to admit them.

■ Apologies can help others forgive you and your mistake, and make it less likely that they will carry a grudge or remain upset.

■ By not offering an apology, you can damage relationships and make future interactions more difficult.

Suggested Activities

Language Arts: Write the following quote from Voltaire on the board or overhead, and then ask students to write their interpretation of the quote in two or three sentences. Have students share their answers aloud, and discuss how this quote relates to skill Steps 4 and 5.

"No snowflake in an avalanche ever feels responsible."

Science/Math: During a unit on DNA, have students research the scientist (James D. Watson) who won a Nobel Prize in 1962 for deciphering the double helix but had his reputation damaged in 2007 because of a controversial remark. Have students research what the scientist said, and why he had to make a public apology. Lead a discussion about whether or not the scientist needed to apologize and if an apology was sufficient in this situation.

Government: Find examples from the world of politics where candidates, office holders or their supporters had to publicly apologize for doing or saying something inappropriate. Have students critique the apologies in terms of sincerity and effectiveness. Ask students how they would apologize if they were in the same situation. For examples of famous apologies, visit perfectapology.com.

Making an Apology (Saying You're Sorry)
Suggested Role-Plays

Teacher Note:

Have students select one of the following scenarios to role-play in class.

1. You argued with your teacher about how she graded your essay. You constantly interrupted her and disrupted the classroom. Following the steps of the skill, show how you would apologize for your behavior.

2. In the cafeteria, you ate lunch with a new group of students. They made fun of one of your friends, who wasn't sitting with you. You didn't defend your friend and even said hurtful things, too. Your friend heard about what you said and is sad and angry. Describe how you would apologize and say you're sorry.

3. Your classroom teacher is out ill, and you have a substitute teacher for the day. When the substitute has her back turned, you make faces and imitate her actions. When she turns around suddenly, she catches you making fun of her. Respond by apologizing and saying you're sorry.

4. You didn't do your chores around the house and were grounded for the weekend. You were so angry, you yelled at your mom and said things you wish you could take back. To repair your relationship with Mom, show and say you're sorry.

5. You were warned not to pass notes in class. You did anyway, got caught and earned an office referral. Show how you would return to the classroom and apologize to the teacher for disrupting the class and not following the rules.

Making an Apology
(Saying You're Sorry)
Think Sheet

Name_____ Date_____

List some times or situations where making an apology and saying you're sorry are important:

-

-

-

-

Why should you learn how to make an apology?

Are there ever times when offering an apology is not necessary? When and why?

When making an apology, what information or details should you include?

-

-

-

-

How can the skill of **Making an Apology (Saying You're Sorry)** help you at school?

How can the skill of **Making an Apology (Saying You're Sorry)** help you at home?

Making an Apology
(Saying You're Sorry)

1. Look at the person.

2. Use a serious, sincere voice tone, but don't pout.

3. Begin by saying, "I wanted to apologize for..." or "I'm sorry for...."

4. Do not make excuses or try to rationalize your behavior.

5. Sincerely say that you will try not to repeat the same behavior in the future.

6. Offer to compensate or pay restitution.

7. Thank the other person for listening.

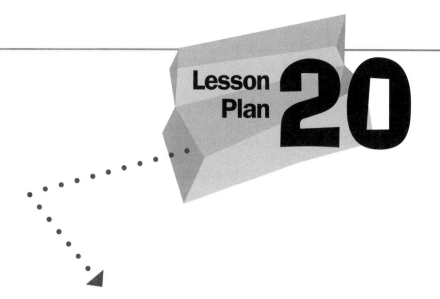

Expressing Empathy and Understanding for Others

Teacher Notes

Some students seem to have little empathy for others. While this is somewhat natural at certain developmental levels, a lack of empathy becomes more pronounced in youth who live in environments that are harsh and aggressive and where empathy is not taught or valued. Fortunately, empathy is a skill that can be learned. Students must first learn how to express empathy – even when they may not feel it – if they are going to internalize this skill. Therefore, it's important that you focus on teaching students how to *show* empathy or understanding rather than how to *feel* empathy or understanding. Empathy has to be internalized, and that involves changing thoughts, feelings and behaviors.

Proactive Teaching Interaction

Introduce the Skill

Have students brainstorm reasons why it is important for them to know how to express empathy and understanding. Reasons can include:

- Builds character

- Strengthens friendships

- Makes others feel better

- Shows kindness

- Others are more likely to return the favor

Describe the Appropriate Behavior or Skill Steps

Expressing Empathy and Understanding for Others

1. **Listen closely as the other person expresses his or her feelings.**

   - Maintain eye contact so you focus on the person and do not get distracted by other people or events around you.

2. **Express empathy by saying, "I understand...."**

3. **Demonstrate concern through your words and actions.**

   - Do not laugh, roll your eyes or act indifferent.

4. **Reflect back the other person's words by saying, "It seems like you're saying...."**

5. **Offer any help or assistance you can.**

Give a Reason or Rationale

Knowing how to express empathy and understanding is a skill that benefits others as much as yourself. There will be times when friends and family members will struggle with problems or experience loss. By being empathetic and understanding, you can ease their stress and help them feel better. Other benefits of knowing how to express empathy and understanding include:

- You strengthen your friendships and relationships.

- You can improve a person's outlook and attitude.

- You build character by showing compassion and concern.

- Others are more likely to reach out and help you when you're hurting.

Suggested Activities

Language Arts: Write the poem *I'm in a Rotten Mood* on the board or overhead. Read the poem aloud, and then ask students how they could show empathy or understanding to someone in such a bad mood. Have students write a poem that communicates empathy to someone feeling glum.

I'm in a Rotten Mood

I'm in a rotten mood today,

A really rotten mood today,

I'm feeling cross,

I'm feeling mean,

I'm jumpy as a jumping bean,

I have an awful attitude –

I'm in a rotten mood!

I'm in a rotten mood today,
A really rotten mood today,
I'm in a snit,
I'm in a stew,
There's nothing that I care to do
But sit all by myself and brood –
I'm in a rotten mood!

I'm in a rotten mood today,
A really rotten mood today,
You'd better stay away from me,
I'm just a lump of misery,
I'm feeling absolutely rude –
I'm in a rotten mood!

Science/Math: Assign a quirky research project by having students find scientific studies about yawning and empathy. Discuss why some researchers believe the more susceptible an individual is to yawning, the more empathetic he or she is. Have students debate whether or not yawning in response to seeing someone else yawn is really an empathetic gesture. Ask them if there are any other behavioral reflexes that could be a sign of empathy.

Geography/History: In a lesson on South Africa, have students research the Truth and Reconciliation Commission that was established after apartheid ended. Lead a discussion about how such a commission provides an opportunity for individuals to express their experiences and feelings and how that can lead to greater understanding and forgiveness.

Government: Bullying is a serious problem in many schools, and research shows that bullies often lack empathy and have difficulty understanding the feelings of others. Have students research whether or not your state has adopted any laws against bullying. If no, discuss whether such a law is needed and what punishment would be appropriate for violating that law. If yes, have students research what the law says and whether anyone has been prosecuted for violating the law.

You also can ask students about the social climate in your school and whether or not they think bullying is a problem. Ask students to describe what rules, policies or procedures they would implement to address bullying and foster a healthier social environment.

Expressing Empathy and Understanding for Others
Suggested Role-Plays

Teacher Note:

Have students select one of the following scenarios to role-play in class.

1. Your friend is very sad because his father died. Show how you would support your friend the first time you see him after the death.

2. Your sister tried out for the lead in the school play but didn't get the part. She is very upset and depressed. Following the steps of the skill, show how you would express empathy and understanding to her.

3. Your best friend's parents are getting a divorce. Your friend is angry and keeps to himself. Show how you would be supportive and understanding.

4. Your classmate flunked the English exam and is feeling frustrated and depressed. Describe how you would express your concern and understanding to him.

5. Your grandparents had to put their beloved pet to sleep. Show how you would be caring and describe what help or assistance you would offer.

Expressing Empathy and Understanding for Others
Think Sheet

Name_____ Date_____

Why should you learn how to be compassionate and show understanding for others?

List some times when a friend may need to be comforted or supported:

-

-

-

-

The second step of this skill is to say something such as, "I understand…." What other words or actions can you say and do to show you care?

-
-
-
-

How can the skill of **Expressing Empathy and Understanding for Others** help you at school?

How can the skill of **Expressing Empathy and Understanding for Others** help you with your family?

Expressing Empathy and Understanding for Others

1. Listen closely as the other person expresses his or her feelings.

2. Express empathy by saying, "I understand...."

3. Demonstrate concern through your words and actions.

4. Reflect back the other person's words by saying, "It seems like you're saying...."

5. Offer any help or assistance you can.

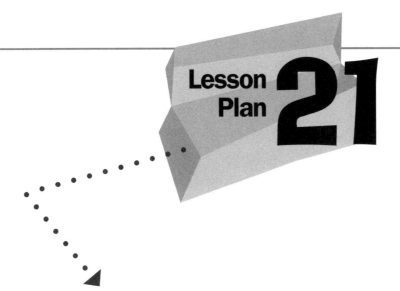

Giving Compliments

Teacher Notes

Compliments, whether given by teachers, administrators or students, help create a warm and positive learning environment. This skill nicely complements the skill of "Accepting Compliments," so both skills can be taught jointly or back to back.

Proactive Teaching Interaction

Introduce the Skill

Have students brainstorm reasons why it is important to know how to compliment others appropriately. Reasons can include:

- Shows your appreciation for hard work or great effort
- Demonstrates thoughtfulness
- Makes others feel better about themselves
- Fosters positive relationships and environments

Describe the Appropriate Behavior or Skill Steps

Giving Compliments

1. **Look at the person you are complimenting.**

   - Eye contact helps communicate your sincerity.

2. **Speak with a clear, enthusiastic voice.**

   - Don't sound condescending or as if you don't mean what you say.

3. **Praise the person's activity or project specifically. Tell him or her exactly what you liked about it.**

   - When you tell someone specifically what you liked, the compliment becomes more meaningful.

4. **Use words such as, "That's great," "Wonderful" or "That was awesome."**

   - Include nonverbal responses, too, such as clapping, shaking hands or smiling.

5. **Give the other person time to respond to your compliment.**

Give a Reason or Rationale

You know how much you like it when someone recognizes your work or praises your effort. However, you can't always expect to be the one hearing compliments. You have to give them, too. Giving compliments is a great way to boost someone's confidence, as well as build relationships. Knowing how to give compliments has many other benefits:

- You can strengthen existing friendships or make new ones.

- You show a willingness to be other-centered rather than self-centered.

- You won't sound insincere or fake, which can hurt someone's feelings.

- Others will be more likely or willing to compliment you.

Suggested Activities

Language Arts: Have students use compliments as conversation starters by writing short, creative fiction stories and then having their stories critiqued by a partner. Students should begin their critiques by first complimenting the writer, and the writer should respond appropriately to the compliment. Students can practice and reinforce the skills of giving AND accepting compliments.

Physical Education: Teach and reinforce the behavioral steps, especially 2, 3 and 4, in the context of the class. Tell students they can earn extra points or a reward by making an appropriate compliment to a player or team. Remind students that the compliment should be genuine and deserving. Examples can include, "Nice shot," "Awesome effort getting to the ball," "Great defense," etc.

History: Prior to oral reports about world leaders, have students practice giving and accepting compliments. Ask students to applaud appropriately after every presentation and make a positive comment to the presenter. The presenter, too, can practice how to accept the compliments by replying graciously.

Giving Compliments
Suggested Role-Plays

Teacher Note:
Have students select one of the following scenarios to role-play in class.

1. Your best friend has been named "Student of the Month." Compliment your friend. (Note: When offering a compliment, you can mention values such as hard work, determination, friendliness, school or community involvement, etc.)

2. While attending the school's art show, you see a beautiful painting by a student you have never met before. Following the steps of the skill, show how you would approach the student and compliment her work.

3. You saw one of your siblings help a disabled person walk through a large crowd. Describe how you would compliment your sibling's caring act.

4. You have a friend who likes to dwell on the negative and always seems to be in a bad mood. One day, you notice that your friend is upbeat and has a real happy outlook. Show how you would praise your friend's cheery attitude.

Giving Compliments
Think Sheet

Name_____ Date_____

Why is it important to learn how to give compliments?

How do you feel after giving someone a compliment?

List some times or situations where it is appropriate to give a compliment:

-

-

-

-

How can the skill of **Giving Compliments** help you in the classroom?

How can the skill of **Giving Compliments** help you outside of school?

Giving Compliments

1. Look at the person you are complimenting.

2. Speak with a clear, enthusiastic voice.

3. Praise the person's activity or project specifically. Tell him or her exactly what you liked about it.

4. Use words such as, "That's great," "Wonderful" or "That was awesome."

5. Give the other person time to respond to your compliment.

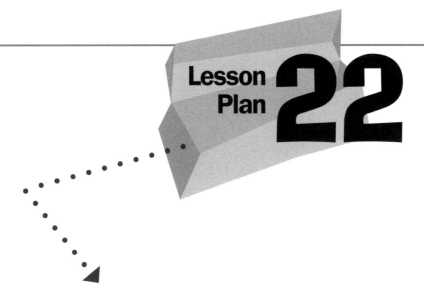

Showing Appreciation

Teacher Notes

Some consider this skill one that's nice for students to have but not essential, especially in an academic setting. However, any learning community that strives to create a warm and welcoming environment needs students who are respectful and display good manners. Teaching students how to show their appreciation can contribute to better social relationships among students and staff.

Proactive Teaching Interaction

Introduce the Skill

You can begin your lesson by handing out a small treat to every student and counting how many say "Thank you." Use students' responses, or non-responses, to start a discussion about being grateful and showing appreciation.

Have students brainstorm reasons why it is important to know how to show appreciation. Reasons can include:

- Contributes to a friendly environment
- Prevents hurt feelings
- Helps maintain friendships
- Shows kindness

Describe the Appropriate Behavior or Skill Steps

Showing Appreciation

1. **Look at the person.**

   ▪ Eye contact communicates your appreciation and sincerity.

2. **Use a pleasant, sincere voice.**

   ▪ Don't mumble or sound sarcastic.

3. **Say "Thank you for..." and specifically describe what the person did that you appreciate.**

4. **If appropriate, give a reason for why it was so beneficial.**

   ▪ Reasons could include how it helps you save money or time, or how it gives you something you never had but always wanted.

5. **Offer future help or favors on your part.**

   ▪ You might say, for example, "Thanks for helping me clean up. Is there anything I can help you with?"

Give a Reason or Rationale

Knowing how to show appreciation is an essential life skill. You will receive kind gestures and gifts of every variety throughout your life. The best and most appropriate response is to be thankful. Showing gratitude to others helps strengthen relationships and contributes to a positive social environment. Other benefits of showing appreciation include:

■ You let others know that what they did was meaningful.

■ You make others feel good about their actions.

■ You are more likely to receive other gifts in the future.

■ You show others that you were deserving of their gift.

Suggested Activities

Language Arts: Ask students to write about an experience where they felt hurt or disappointed because they were generous toward someone but the individual did not seem grateful. Have students include a description of how they wish the person had shown his or her appreciation.

Family and Consumer Sciences: Have students show their appreciation to the community in which they live by doing a service or volunteer project.

Opportunities, such as visiting nursing homes, collecting donations for a food pantry, building homes for Habitat for Humanity, assisting with a literacy project or volunteering at an animal shelter, provide a unique way of showing appreciation to others.

Government/Social Studies: Have students research the different ways the United States government expresses its appreciation to citizens, and then have them write a report explaining the history and meaning of an award or honor. Examples can include the Presidential Medal of Freedom, the Medal of Honor and the Presidential Citizens Medal.

Showing Appreciation
Suggested Role-Plays

Teacher Note:
Have students select one of the following scenarios to role-play in class.

1. On Valentine's Day, many classmates give you treats. Following the steps of the skill, show your appreciation.

2. Your friends make a giant birthday card and give you a gag gift for your birthday. Describe how you would show your thanks.

3. Your grandmother buys you a video game, but it is one that you played before and didn't like. Describe how you would be kind and thank her for the gift.

4. You trip and fall in the hallway, and your books scatter across the floor. A student you do not know stops and helps pick up your belongings. Show your appreciation.

5. Your friend's dad buys you an ice cream cone after a ballgame. Without using the words "Thank you," describe how you can say or show your appreciation.

Showing Appreciation
Think Sheet

Name_____ Date _____

Why is it important to know how to show appreciation?

List some times or places where you can expect to receive gifts or favors:

-

-

-

-

How should you look and sound when you show appreciation or say "Thank you"?

In addition to saying "Thank you," what other words or actions can you say and do to show your appreciation?

-

-

-

-

How can you show your appreciation to performers, presenters and others during…

- sporting events?

- recitals?

- award banquets?

How can using the skill of **Showing Appreciation** help you at school?

How can using the skill of **Showing Appreciation** help you at work or home?

Showing Appreciation

1. **Look at the person.**

2. **Use a pleasant, sincere voice.**

3. **Say "Thank you for..." and specifically describe what the person did that you appreciate.**

4. **If appropriate, give a reason for why it was so beneficial.**

5. **Offer future help or favors on your part.**

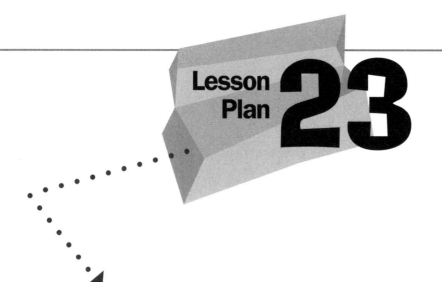

Accepting Awards
and Honors

Teacher Notes

Many students struggle with this skill. Some are uncomfortable with public attention and are unsure of how to accept the recognition without "standing out" too much. For others, the reverse is true. Some students, such as class clowns, seek attention and use formal events (graduation, honors banquet, etc.) as opportunities to goof off and get laughs. The best time to teach and review this skill is before any event in which students will be recognized, including assemblies, banquets and graduations.

Proactive Teaching Interaction

Introduce the Skill

Ask students to describe any experiences they've had accepting awards and honors in public, or to recall any memorable moments they've witnessed, either in person or on television, of people accepting awards and honors. Have them describe what was good and/or bad about the behavior of the honoree(s).

Have students brainstorm reasons why it is important to know how to accept an award or honor graciously. Reasons can include:

- Shows maturity
- Shows graciousness
- Demonstrates sincerity
- Prevents hurt feelings

■ Shows respect to the presenter

■ Shows respect to other nominees and family and friends in the audience

Describe the Appropriate Behavior or Skill Steps

Accepting Awards and Honors

1. **Look at the presenter.**

   ▪ Hold your head up and make eye contact with the presenter, as well as with the audience.

2. **Shake hands.**

   ▪ Use a firm grip.

3. **Maintain a pleasant facial expression.**

   ▪ A smile communicates to everyone that you are happy to be there.

4. **Use a pleasant voice tone and say, "Thank you for..." or "I feel honored."**

   ▪ Do not use inappropriate language.

5. **Return quietly to your seat.**

   ▪ Avoid boastful behaviors, such as using your hands to signal louder or longer applause.

Give a Reason or Rationale

Whenever you are recognized for your performance or an accomplishment, it is appropriate to show appreciation and thanks. When you accept awards and honors in a humble and sincere manner, you show others that you are gracious and polite. Those behaviors reflect well on you, your family and your school. Other benefits of knowing how to appropriately accept awards and honors include:

■ Others will see that you are deserving of the recognition.

■ You will respect the feelings of those who did not "win," as well as their friends and family.

■ Others will see you as someone who is kind and grateful.

■ You show respect to the individual or organization that is honoring you.

Suggested Activities

Language Arts: Legendary actor Marlon Brando famously refused to accept the Oscar he won for his performance in *The Godfather*. Instead, an actress dressed in traditional Native American clothes walked on stage and read a statement from Brando protesting the unfair treatment of Native Americans. Have students debate whether or not this was an appropriate response after winning such a prestigious honor, and then ask students to write and deliver their own Oscar acceptance speeches.

Science/Math: Show a video clip of a mathematician or scientist accepting a Nobel Prize or National Medal of Science award. Ask students to describe what they liked or didn't like about what the honoree said when accepting the award. Have students choose a science or math subject (preferably one they have studied so this exercise can be a review) and pretend they developed the idea or made the discovery and will be accepting a prestigious award. Have students accept their "award" and give an acceptance speech in class.

Accepting Awards and Honors
Suggested Role-Plays

Teacher Note:
Have students select one of the following scenarios to role-play in class.

1. You are one of seven students who earned a certificate for perfect attendance. Following the steps of the skill, show how you would accept the certificate from the principal.

2. You earned the "Most Improved Player" award. At the sports banquet, you will receive a plaque and have time to say a few words. Show how you would graciously accept the honor and include words of thanks.

3. You earned "Student of the Month" and are called up to the stage during the all-school assembly. Show how you would walk to the podium and accept the honor.

4. You were just announced the winner of the state speech contest. Show how to accept the award graciously.

5. You are graduating from school. Show how you would walk across the stage to accept your diploma from the principal or school board president.

Accepting Awards and Honors
Think Sheet

Name_____ Date _____

Why is it important to know how to accept awards and honors?

List some times or places where this skill will be helpful to you:

-

-

-

-

When you are given an award, what words or phrases can you say to show others how happy you are to receive the award?

-

-

-

-

How can the skill of **Accepting Awards and Honors** help you at school?

Outside of school, where and when is it important or necessary to follow the steps of this skill?

Accepting Awards and Honors

1. Look at the presenter.

2. Shake hands.

3. Maintain a pleasant facial expression.

4. Use a pleasant voice tone and say, "Thank you for..." or "I feel honored."

5. Return quietly to your seat.

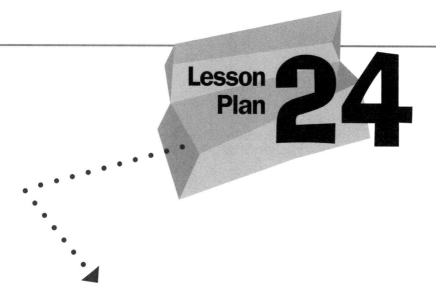

Accepting Compliments

Teacher Notes

This seemingly simple skill is one that too many students (and adults) lack. Most individuals do not want to be perceived as arrogant or conceited, so they will downplay or dismiss compliments without so much as a "Thank you." As mentioned earlier, this skill should be taught in conjunction with, or immediately after, the skill of "Giving Compliments."

Proactive Teaching Interaction

Introduce the Skill

Ask students to describe their feelings when they receive a compliment, and whether they react differently when it comes from a friend, teacher or stranger. Also ask students if they ever offered a compliment to someone who then ignored or dismissed their praise, and how that made them feel. Use their experiences to brainstorm reasons why it is important to accept compliments graciously. Reasons can include:

- Shows appreciation

- Improves the social climate of the classroom and school

- Encourages others to offer compliments or be more accepting of criticisms

- Lets the other person know you care about how he or she feels about you

Describe the Appropriate Behavior or Skill Steps

Accepting Compliments

1. **Look at the person who is complimenting you.**

   ▪ Eye contact is one way to communicate your appreciation and thanks.

2. **Use a pleasant voice tone.**

   ▪ Don't use a tone that sounds indifferent or ungrateful.

3. **Thank the person sincerely for the compliment.**

4. **Say "Thanks for noticing" or "I appreciate that."**

5. **Avoid looking away, mumbling or denying the compliment.**

Give a Reason or Rationale

Whenever you invest a lot of time and effort in a project, or try to do what's right, it feels good to have someone notice. Hearing a kind word lets you know that your work isn't taken for granted. However, you sometimes may feel uncomfortable receiving a compliment or be dismissive toward whoever offered it. Discounting a compliment can be like putting yourself down, and it can be disrespectful to the person who offered the praise. Knowing how to accept compliments has many benefits:

■ You show others that you are mature, confident and deserving of their praise.

■ Others will likely compliment you again, knowing that you appreciate their support.

■ You show that you value the person's kind words and opinion.

■ You won't make others feel like their words don't matter.

Suggested Activities

Language Arts: Ask students to write about a time when they did not accept a compliment because they thought it was insincere or mean-spirited. Have them describe why they felt that way, and how they would react if it happened again.

Science/Math: Have students research the National Academy of Sciences (NAS) and its members. Ask students to select one scientist or engineer and write an essay describing what he or she did to earn membership in this exclusive club. Ask students to explain why being elected into the NAS is a compliment that is rarely, if ever, refused.

Physical Education: Ask students to share stories about moments when they complimented a competitor for winning or playing hard. Lead a discussion about how people respond to compliments, and why sometimes downplaying or dismissing someone's statement of congratulations can be a sign of poor sportsmanship.

Accepting Compliments
Suggested Role-Plays

Teacher Note:

Have students select one of the following scenarios to role-play in class.

1. Players from the losing team compliment you for your energy and enthusiasm. Show how you would politely accept their praise.

2. You hate the outfit you are wearing, but a teacher tells you that it looks nice. Following the steps of the skill, show how to accept the compliment.

3. You worked all night building your science project. In the morning, your parents say "Nice job." You are a little disappointed that they didn't seem more impressed. Show how you would accept their compliment anyway.

4. After meeting your family for the first time, your friends tell you how lucky you are to have such "cool" parents. You are embarrassed and don't consider your parents to be cool. Show how you would accept their "compliment" anyway.

Accepting Compliments
Think Sheet

Name_____ Date _____

What compliments mean the most to you?

List some words or phrases you can say to someone that shows you heard the compliment and appreciate what he or she said:

-
-
-
-

Why is it important to know how to accept a compliment from others?

How can the skill of **Accepting Compliments** help you in the classroom?

How can the skill of **Accepting Compliments** help you outside of school?

196

Accepting Compliments

1. **Look at the person who is complimenting you.**

2. **Use a pleasant voice tone.**

3. **Thank the person sincerely for the compliment.**

4. **Say "Thanks for noticing" or "I appreciate that."**

5. **Avoid looking away, mumbling or denying the compliment.**

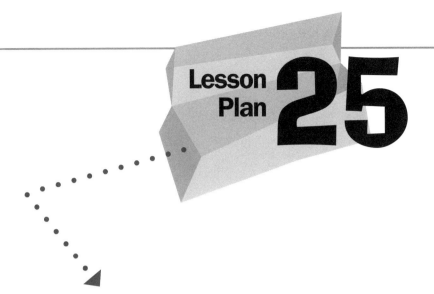

Going to an Assembly

Teacher Notes

A school-specific skill such as this should be taught in context. In other words, teach this skill by having students line up in the classroom, walk quietly in the hallway and take their seats in the auditorium or gymnasium.

Proactive Teaching Interaction

Introduce the Skill

In the auditorium, have students brainstorm reasons why it's important for them to know how to go to an assembly. Reasons can include:

- Limits rowdiness
- Shows respect
- Allows the assembly to start on time
- Sets a good example for other students
- Prevents them from getting into trouble

Describe the Appropriate Behavior or Skill Steps

Going to an Assembly

1. **Walk quietly in the hallway.**

   - Don't stomp your feet, shout or bang against the walls or lockers. By limiting disruptions, everyone stays on schedule.

2. **Sit in your assigned seat (or section).**

   ▪ Don't create confusion by moving from spot to spot or blocking others from their seats.

3. **Listen attentively.**

   ▪ Be respectful and pay attention. Don't engage in conversations when others are speaking or performing.

4. **Clap at an appropriate time, in an appropriate manner.**

   ▪ Show your appreciation.

5. **Wait to be dismissed.**

   ▪ Don't head to the exits early or stampede out of the auditorium.

Give a Reason or Rationale

Assemblies occur periodically throughout the school year, so it's important that you know how to conduct yourself at these events. Sometimes, students think assemblies are a time to goof off or not pay attention. However, a school assembly is basically a giant classroom, and the same behavioral expectations apply. Knowing how to go to an assembly has many benefits:

■ You will a set a good example for other students.

■ You won't get in trouble for inappropriate behavior.

■ You can learn something new when you pay attention to the speaker or performance.

■ You contribute to a positive and healthy learning environment.

■ You show respect to others in the audience, as well as to the presenters.

Suggested Activities

As an educator, you naturally put students in situations that require them to use various social skills. In addition to blending social skills instruction with academic instruction, you also can incorporate the teaching of social skills with specific academic tasks, such as going to an assembly. The following examples highlight opportunities for teaching social skills based on what is happening in the classroom.

Language Arts: Prior to a speech contest, explain your behavioral expectations (speakers stand at the front of the room, audience sits quietly and listens, be respectful and applaud after each presentation).

Science/Math: Prior to the school science fair, explain the procedure and what students need to do (when to arrive, what to wear, where to set up, what questions to expect from visitors and judges and how projects will be judged).

Government/History: Prior to a visit from a guest lecturer, explain your behavioral expectations (greet the visitor, listen intently, ask questions when appropriate and applaud appropriately at the conclusion of the presentation.)

Group Role-Play

To role-play this skill, we recommend doing a group exercise that allows students an opportunity to demonstrate or describe how the skill can be used during a variety of school-related events and activities.

As a group, show appropriate and socially acceptable ways to act when attending…

- An all-school pep rally

- An outdoor football game

- An indoor volleyball match

- A concert

- A school musical

- A school speech contest

- An awards banquet

- A classroom presentation by a guest speaker

Going to an Assembly
Think Sheet

Name_____ Date _____

Outside of school, where and when is it important or necessary to follow the steps of this skill?

One step of the skill is to clap at an appropriate time, in an appropriate manner. What are other appropriate responses or reactions if you are attending a…

- sporting event?

- pep rally?

- music concert?

- play or recital?

How can the skill of **Going to an Assembly** help you at school?

How can the skill of **Going to an Assembly** help you outside of school?

Going to an Assembly

1. Walk quietly in the hallway.

2. Sit in your assigned seat (or section).

3. Listen attentively.

4. Clap at an appropriate time, in an appropriate manner.

5. Wait to be dismissed.

Accepting Winning Appropriately

Teacher Notes

Media saturate the lives of most students, and as a result, they are often exposed to images of sports celebrities. Unfortunately, some of these celebrities are as famous for talking smack and taunting opponents as they are for their athletic accomplishments. These athletes are role models, but too often their behaviors are not what you want your students to emulate in the classroom, on the playground or on the field of play. The skill of "Accepting Winning Appropriately" can be a counterweight to the many unsportsmanlike messages young people see and hear.

Proactive Teaching Interaction

Introduce the Skill

Introduce the skill by showing video clips of college or professional athletes celebrating their victories. Ask students to identify any behaviors that are appropriate and show good sportsmanship.

Have students brainstorm reasons why it is important to know how to accept winning appropriately. Reasons can include:

- Makes the losing team or players feel better
- Shows respect
- Avoids penalties for poor sportsmanship
- Helps maintain friendships or relationships

Describe the Appropriate Behavior or Skill Steps

Accepting Winning Appropriately

1. **Look at the person or members of the team who lost.**

   - Eye contact shows respect; don't "stare down" or ignore your opponent(s).

2. **Remain pleasant but not overly happy or celebratory.**

   - When celebrating a victory, it's okay for you to congratulate your teammates with pats on the back, smiles, high-fives, hugs, etc.

   - Don't showoff, gloat or taunt the losing team or player.

3. **Congratulate the other person or team for a good game and for trying.**

   - Sound sincere; don't mumble.

   - Say something like, "Great effort" or "Good game."

4. **Do not brag or boast about winning.**

Give a Reason or Rationale

Being a gracious winner is sometimes difficult, especially after beating a bitter rival or winning a highly emotional or competitive match. It's hard to be humble when you put forth a great effort or are on a winning streak. Real winners, however, do not gloat or belittle their competition. Instead, they demonstrate good sportsmanship and maturity by applauding their competitors' efforts. Knowing how to win graciously has many benefits:

- Winning graciously can help you maintain friendships and relationships.

- Gloating and bragging is not appreciated by others and can hurt friendships.

- Other teams, players, coaches and officials will form a good opinion of you, your team and school.

- Others will want you on their team or will want to compete against you because of your positive attitude.

- Winning graciously shows respect for the hard work and effort of your opponent.

Suggested Activities

Language Arts: Have students read Stephen Hoffius's *Winners and Losers* (grades 4-8), E.L. Konigsburg's *The View from Saturday* (grades 3-6), Rich

Wallace's *Wrestling Sturbridge* (grades 7-12) or another age-appropriate story about competition and fair play. Have students write an essay about how a character dealt with the pressure or expectation to win, and if the character is a good or bad role model.

Physical Education: Teach and reinforce the skill in the context of the class. Prior to any game between individuals or teams, review the skill steps, as well as the skill steps of "Accepting Defeat or Loss." Praise students when they display good sportsmanship.

History: During a unit on World War II, write the following quote from Jesse Owens on the board or overhead. Ask students to explain how his words relate to the concept of being a gracious winner, and then discuss how Owens's accomplishments at the 1936 Olympics undermined the Nazi Party's propaganda effort promoting Aryan superiority.

"In the end, it's extra effort that separates a winner from second place. But winning takes a lot more than that, too. It starts with complete command of the fundamentals. Then it takes desire, determination, discipline and self-sacrifice. And finally, it takes a great deal of love, fairness and respect for your fellow man. Put all these together, and even if you don't win, how can you lose?"

Accepting Winning Appropriately
Suggested Role-Plays

Teacher Note:

Have students select one of the following scenarios to role-play in class.

1. Your soccer team is ahead by two goals when the recess bell sounds, so your team wins the match. Following the steps of the skill, show how to celebrate the victory.

2. You have just beaten the defending checkers champion. She is visibly sad and upset. Show how to be a gracious winner.

3. You participate in the school's speech contest and deliver the best speech of the day. Everyone claps and tells you what a great job you did. Show how to appropriately accept their praise.

4. Your teacher tells the class that you earned the highest score on the math test. Show how to accept this "win" graciously.

5. Your basketball team scores a basket at the buzzer to win the game. You and your teammates celebrate wildly. Show how to enjoy the victory while being respectful to the losing team.

6. You just beat your bitter rival in a tennis match. Describe behaviors that show poor sportsmanship, and then show how to be a gracious winner.

Accepting Winning Appropriately
Think Sheet

Name_____ Date _____

How does winning make you feel?

What can you say or do to show that you are a good sport after winning a game or contest?

-

-

-

-

How can the skill of **Accepting Winning Appropriately** help you at school?

How can the skill of **Accepting Winning Appropriately** help your school or team?

Accepting Winning Appropriately

1. **Look at the person or members of the team who lost.**

2. **Remain pleasant but not overly happy or celebratory.**

3. **Congratulate the other person or team for a good game and for trying.**

4. **Do not brag or boast about winning.**

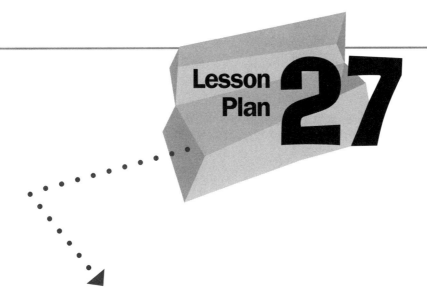

Accepting Defeat or Loss

Teacher Notes

As we all know, defeat is difficult to accept sometimes. It is disappointing and frustrating to work hard and come up short. Sadly, too many students express their disappointment by making excuses, arguing, acting surly or being dismissive and disrespectful to the winners, officials and opposing fans. All of these behaviors have a negative impact on a learning community's social environment.

Proactive Teaching Interaction

Introduce the Skill

Ask students if they have ever witnessed a team, player, coach or fan react inappropriately to a defeat. Have students describe the situation and how it made them feel. Also ask students to describe any times when they saw a team, player, coach or fan accept a loss with grace and sportsmanship. Discuss the behaviors they saw and the words they heard.

Have students brainstorm reasons why it is important to know how to accept defeat or loss. Reasons can include:

- Shows respect to the winners, players, coaches and fans

- Demonstrates maturity

- Helps foster a healthy environment for competition

- Sets a good example for younger athletes

Describe the Appropriate Behavior or Skill Steps

Accepting Defeat or Loss

1. **Look at the person or members of the team who won.**
   - Don't glare at, sneer at or stare down the winner(s).

2. **Remain calm and positive.**
   - Don't scream in anger or pout.

3. **Say "Good game" or "Congratulations."**
   - Use a pleasant or neutral voice tone; avoid sounding insincere or sarcastic.

4. **Reward yourself for trying your hardest.**
   - Do something fun with friends or family, or indulge in a favorite food.

Give a Reason or Rationale

Losing can be difficult to accept, but everyone experiences defeat in life. How you respond to a loss or setback is what really matters. Real "winners" are those who can be gracious in defeat and carry on. Knowing how to accept a defeat or loss has many benefits:

- You don't allow yourself to wallow in bitterness or sadness.

- You show maturity and resiliency.

- Others will want to compete against you because they know you won't get angry or jealous if things don't go your way.

- You contribute to your school's or team's reputation of good sportsmanship.

Suggested Activities

Language Arts: Have students watch John Avildsen's *Rocky* (PG), David Anspaugh's *Rudy* (PG) or any age-appropriate movie or television program about handling defeat or dealing with obstacles. Discuss how a film's characters cope with setbacks and disappointments. Have students write an essay about how they can turn adversity or loss into an opportunity to achieve future success.

You also can write the following quote from Malcolm X on the board or overhead. Read the quote aloud, and then ask students to explain its meaning and how his words can apply to their own lives.

"There is no better teacher than adversity. Every defeat, every heartbreak, every loss, contains its own seed, its own lesson on how to improve your performance the next time."

Science/Math: Have students compete in a student stock market competition by researching companies and then investing make-believe money in the market. Let them track their investments over a period of several weeks or months. When the value of a stock falls, discuss how they feel about losing money and the risks of making rash decisions or responding emotionally to the market's ups and downs.

Government/History: Have students research the presidential election of 2000 or any hotly contested campaign at the local or state level. Ask students to find articles or images from a campaign that discuss or depict the reactions from individuals on the losing side. Discuss how individuals dealt with the defeat and whether their responses were gracious or not. You also can write the following excerpt from Al Gore's concession speech on the board or overhead (an entire transcript is available from multiple online sources), and ask students to explain how his words relate to skill Steps 2 and 3.

"I've seen America in this campaign, and I like what I see. It's worth fighting for and that's a fight I'll never stop. As for the battle that ends tonight, I do believe, as my father once said, that 'No matter how hard the loss, defeat might serve as well as victory to shape the soul and let the glory out.'"

Physical Education: Teach and reinforce the skill in the context of the class. Prior to any game between individuals or teams, review the skill steps, as well as the skill steps of "Accepting Winning Appropriately." Praise students when they display good sportsmanship.

Accepting Defeat or Loss
Suggested Role-Plays

Teacher Note:

Have students select one of the following scenarios to role-play in class.

1. Your soccer team was behind by one goal when the recess bell rang, and your team lost. Following the steps of the skill, show how you would be respectful to the winning team as you all walk back to class.

2. For the second year in a row, you are the runner-up in the school spelling bee. Show how you would congratulate the winner and accept the defeat.

3. Your basketball team loses at the buzzer, denying your team a trip to the state tournament. Describe behaviors that show poor sportsmanship and are inappropriate after a defeat, and then show how you would congratulate the winning team.

4. You are competing against your bitter rival in a track meet. As you are about to cross the finish line in first place, you trip on your shoelace and fall down. Your rival passes you, wins the race and celebrates wildly. Show how you would be a good sport after experiencing such a heartbreaking defeat.

Accepting Defeat or Loss
Think Sheet

Name_____ Date_____

How does losing make you feel?

When is it hard for you to accept a defeat or loss, and why? What positive things can you do to deal with your disappointment?

Why is it important to know how to accept a defeat or loss?

What can you say or do to show good sportsmanship after a loss?

-
-
-
-

How can the skill of **Accepting Defeat or Loss** help you at school?

How can the skill of **Accepting Defeat or Loss** help your team?

Accepting Defeat or Loss

1. Look at the person or members of the team who won.

2. Remain calm and positive.

3. Say "Good game" or "Congratulations."

4. Reward yourself for trying your hardest.

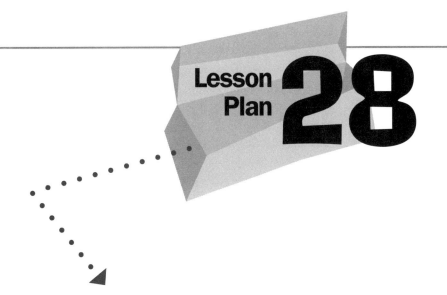

Choosing Appropriate Friends

Teacher Notes

In your learning community, you want everyone to have friendship skills. Even though you can't expect all students to be or become friends, it's important that they at least learn how to be friendly toward one another. The more students can get along or tolerate one another, the less likely they are to fight, argue, bully and harass.

The answer to the question of who is an "appropriate" friend is very subjective. When teaching this lesson, it's helpful if you avoid labeling specific students or groups of students as "inappropriate." Rather, emphasize the positive attributes and potential benefits of associating with individuals who are a good influence. Someone who is a positive influence shows respect to others, works hard in school, follows the rules and tries to do the right thing. Point out to students that when they hang around with individuals who have those characteristics or hold those values, they, too, can become better people and friends.

Proactive Teaching Interaction

Introduce the Skill

Ask students to think about their own friendships and then write down any qualities or characteristics their friends have in common. Ask for volunteers to share their answers aloud and then discuss what makes someone a good friend.

You also can have students brainstorm reasons why choosing appropriate friends is important. Reasons can include:

- Makes life easier and more enjoyable
- Helps keep you away from bad influences
- Provides you with a sense of emotional and physical security
- Shows maturity

Describe the Appropriate Behavior or Skill Steps

Choosing Appropriate Friends

1. **Think of the qualities and interests you would look for in a friend.**
   - "Qualities" refer to personality traits, such as humor, honesty, being easygoing, etc.
   - "Interests" refer to things someone enjoys, such as playing sports or video games, singing, shopping, reading spy novels, etc.

2. **Look at the strengths and weaknesses of potential friends.**
   - Strengths can be values such as trustworthiness, respect, cooperation and caring.
   - Weaknesses are characteristics or traits that show a lack of values, such as dishonesty or being disrespectful, selfish or uncaring.

3. **Match the characteristics of potential friends with activities and interests you would share.**
   - If you enjoy playing sports, for example, a potential friend would be someone who plays fair, displays good sportsmanship and stays positive even in defeat.
   - If you enjoy volunteering in the community, for example, a potential friend would be someone who is respectful, dependable and giving.

4. **Avoid peers who are involved with drugs, gangs or breaking the law.**

Give a Reason or Rationale

Knowing how to develop friendships and choosing the right friends can have a significant impact on your life. A good friend can help you overcome obstacles, ease disappointment and be a source of strength. A good friend will listen to you, laugh with you and let you know the truth, even when it hurts.

Other benefits of choosing appropriate friends include:

■ You are less likely to be asked, or pressured, to do things – steal, cheat or lie – that are wrong or go against your values.

■ You surround yourself with people who will have your back, motivate you, support you through the rough times and celebrate your successes.

■ You enjoy life more because you're sharing experiences with people who share similar interests and who want to spend time with you.

Suggested Activities

Language Arts: Have students read John Steinbeck's *Of Mice and Men* (grades 10-12), Louis Sachar's *Holes* (grades 6-8), Katherine Paterson's *Bridge to Terabithia* (grades 5-9) or any age-appropriate novel with a plot that emphasizes human relationships. Have students write a one-page report that explains the various friendships depicted in the story and how those friendships influenced, for better or worse, the actions of the characters.

Social Studies/American History: Write the following quotes on the board or overhead. Have students write a paragraph or two explaining how each quote reflects the essence of the individuals, the times in which they lived or the circumstances of their lives. If students are unfamiliar with any individual(s), provide appropriate biographical information or replace the quoted individual with a regional, national or international figure students have studied.

■ "Walking with a friend in the dark is better than walking alone in the light."
- *Helen Keller*

■ "Am I not destroying my enemies when I make friends of them?"
- *Abraham Lincoln*

■ "Friendship with oneself is all-important, because without it one cannot be friends with anyone else in the world."
- *Eleanor Roosevelt*

Group Role-Play

This is a teacher-directed group role-play and requires more instruction and direction. You may need to modify these instructions to accurately reflect the size of your class, the developmental level of your students and the amount of time available.

Begin by asking students to follow the steps of the skill to create a list of characteristics they think a good friend should possess. Have several students share their answers aloud, and write their responses on the board or overhead. Then ask students to create a second list of characteristics or traits that make someone an inappropriate friend. Again, have several students share their answers aloud, and record their responses on the board or overhead. From the two lists you recorded, choose several traits and write them on separate flash-cards (two or three traits per card.)

Have students pair up for the role-play. One student plays the part of the "new student" and another plays the "possible friend." Give the "possible friend" one of the flashcards you've prepared. Have the "new student" introduce himself or herself to the "possible friend" using the skill of "Greeting Others." (This role-play is an opportunity to review skills already taught to students.) The "possible friend" should respond to the greeting by verbally stating or acting out the characteristics that are written on his or her flashcard.

Here is an example of what an interaction might look and sound like:

New Student (extends hand and says): "Good morning. My name is _____, and I'm a new student."

Possible Friend (looks at new student and says): "Good morning. My name is _____, and I'm trustworthy, loyal and friendly."

After the greeting, the "new student" has to decide if the "possible friend" would be a good friend to have. If yes, the "new student" should engage the "possible friend" in a conversation, talking about their interests, hobbies or likes and dislikes. If the answer is no, the "new student" should explain to the class why the friendship would be inappropriate.

If time allows, have students rotate roles so everyone has a chance to play the "new student" and "possible friend." To make the role-plays more challenging and reflective of real life, create flashcards that have both positive and negative traits ("truthful," "helpful" and "greedy"). This will force students to decide what they value most in their friendships and what they can and cannot tolerate from others. You also can have a "new student" approach a group of "possible friends," with each group member displaying good or bad characteristics or a combination of both.

Choosing Appropriate Friends
Think Sheet

Name_____ Date _____

List the qualities or traits that you think make a good friend:

-

-

-

-

Why is it better to be friends with someone who is caring and does the right thing than someone who does not have or show those qualities?

Do you have any friends who make you feel uncomfortable or insecure? If yes, what makes you feel that way and what can you do to change the relationship?

How can the skill of **Choosing Appropriate Friends** help you at school?

How can the skill of **Choosing Appropriate Friends** help you outside of school?

Choosing Appropriate Friends

1. **Think of the qualities and interests you would look for in a friend.**

2. **Look at the strengths and weaknesses of potential friends.**

3. **Match the characteristics of potential friends with activities and interests you would share.**

4. **Avoid peers who are involved with drugs, gangs or breaking the law.**

Setting Appropriate Boundaries

Teacher Notes

Before students can develop healthy relationships with others, they need to understand the importance of creating appropriate boundaries, or a "safe space," that protects their bodies, thoughts and feelings. Students whose boundaries are too open can be victimized physically and emotionally. Likewise, if their boundaries are too closed, relationships and friendships can never fully develop.

In this lesson, it's important to define what physical and emotional boundaries are and how different kinds of relationships should have different kinds of boundaries. For example, the physical and emotional boundaries students have with their siblings or parents should feel and look different from the boundaries they have with friends, classmates and you.

Proactive Teaching Interaction

Introduce the Skill

Begin by defining and explaining the term "boundaries." Define boundaries as the limits we set in our relationships that define what is acceptable or unacceptable. Physical boundaries, for example, protect us and help us decide how and by whom we can be touched. Emotional boundaries protect our thoughts and emotions and help us decide what feelings we will share and with whom.

To help make the concept of boundaries more concrete for students, ask them to imagine a series of circles around their physical and emotional selves. Or, have students draw their own boundary circles by writing the word "Self" in the middle of a sheet of paper and drawing several circles around the word. Explain that each circle represents how close they will allow others to get to them. The circles closest to their physical and emotional selves are the most intimate boundaries and are appropriate for the people who are dearest to them, such as close family members and best friends. The circles that are farthest away represent boundaries that are appropriate for superficial or extremely superficial relationships, such as with an acquaintance, classmate or stranger.

Describe the Appropriate Behavior or Skill Steps

Setting Appropriate Boundaries

1. **Imagine a series of circles radiating out from you. Each represents a boundary.**

   - The relationships you have and everyone you encounter fits somewhere in these boundary circles. Strangers should be in the farthest outside circle while your family and closest friends should be in your inner circles. Classmates, teachers and neighbors should fall in the middle circles.

2. **Picture people you encounter in one of the circles, depending on the level of closeness with which you and another person are comfortable.**

   - Evaluate your relationships. As you think about each person, ask yourself what boundary is most appropriate. Should the person be closer to you, farther away or where he or she is?

3. **Disclose personal information only to those in the closest boundaries.**

   - Before sharing your thoughts and feelings with someone, consider your relationship with him or her. How long have you known the person? How much personal information have you already shared? How much has the other person shared with you? Are you comfortable with the sharing? Can you trust the person?

   - When you are just getting to know someone, you should share small bits of personal information, something you really wouldn't mind others finding out about.

4. **Touch and talk to others only in ways that are appropriate to your boundaries. Also, respect the boundaries of others.**

   - Maintain balance in all your relationships. A relationship is not healthy if one person uses or manipulates the other. Relationships should make you feel safe and comfortable. If you don't feel this way, why not?

- Remember that all relationships change; some change for the better and some for the worse.

- Follow the Golden Rule by treating others as you want them to treat you.

Give a Reason or Rationale

When you set appropriate boundaries for the various relationships you have in your life, you protect your physical and emotional well-being. Good boundaries also help you develop friendships and relationships that are rooted in respect and more likely to last. Other benefits of having appropriate boundaries include:

- You earn the trust and respect of others.

- You keep yourself from getting used or abused, yet you do not isolate yourself from others.

- You learn how and when to stand up for yourself.

- You are able to be in relationships without losing your own identity.

- You are more likely to surround yourself with people who are trustworthy and respectful.

Suggested Activities

Language Arts: Write the poem *Can We Be Friends* by Sara Holbrook on the board or an overhead. Read the poem aloud, and then ask students to interpret the poem from the perspective of relationships and boundaries. (There are no "right" or "wrong" answers.) Have students write an original poem about boundaries and friendships.

Can We Be Friends

I had an overview
of little bits
of all of you.
I circle for a place to land.
Trying to find the best approach,
looking casual
unplanned.
I'm not up for showing off
And I don't want to pretend.
No high-flying aerobatics –
I just want to be your friend.

Science/Math: Relate the issue of personal boundaries to plate tectonics. Have students research the relationship between earthquakes and plate boundaries. Ask students to make connections between the consequences of violating someone's personal space and the collision of tectonic plates.

Geography/Social Studies: Kashmir and the West Bank are two regions of the world where border and boundary disputes have led to violence and unrest. Have students do mini-research projects on one or both of these regions (or any similar disputes in modern or ancient history). Ask them to identify the origins of the dispute, countries or peoples involved and what, if any, resolution was achieved. After they present their projects, have students discuss how the causes and consequences of violating physical borders can be similar to those of violations of personal boundaries.

Boundaries Role-Play

This is a teacher-directed role-play and requires more instruction and observation. You may need to modify these instructions to accurately reflect the size of your class, the developmental level of your students and the amount of time available.

Start by asking two volunteers to come to the front of the room. Have them stand several feet apart, facing each other. Designate one volunteer to play the "stranger" and the other to play "self." Ask "self" to stay in his or her spot and be silent during the role-play. Tell the "stranger" to walk toward "self" and keep walking until "self" gives a nonverbal sign to stop. Instruct the rest of the students to watch the interaction and note what nonverbal signs "self" uses to tell the "stranger" to stop, and how close the "stranger" is allowed to get to "self." When the exercise is over, ask students to discuss what they observed. Repeat the exercise again, but secretly tell the "stranger" to ignore the stop signals from "self" and to keep walking. Again, have the other students observe the behaviors and reactions of the two volunteers. Discuss how the behaviors and reactions differed when the physical boundaries were respected and when they were violated.

Setting Appropriate Boundaries
Think Sheet

Name_____ Date _____

Are the relationship boundaries you have with your friends different from the boundaries you have with teachers and school staff? If so, how?

What are some ways an individual might violate or ignore your boundaries?

If someone is constantly violating your boundaries, how does that make you feel and what should you do?

How does violating someone else's personal boundaries affect you?

What can you do to make amends or apologize for violating the boundaries of others?

How can the skill of **Setting Appropriate Boundaries** help you at school?

How can the skill of **Setting Appropriate Boundaries** help you at home or work?

Setting Appropriate Boundaries

1. Imagine a series of circles radiating out from you. Each represents a boundary.

2. Picture people you encounter in one of the circles, depending on the level of closeness with which you and another person are comfortable.

3. Disclose personal information only to those in the closest boundaries.

4. Touch and talk to others only in ways that are appropriate to your boundaries. Also, respect the boundaries of others.

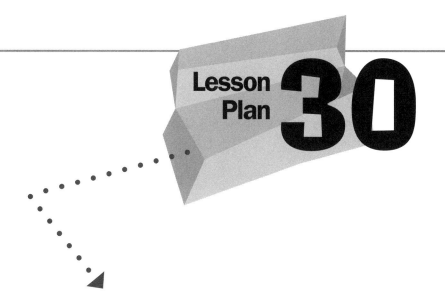

Extending an Offer or Invitation

Teacher Notes

This lesson is a natural complement to the skill of "Declining an Offer or Invitation Graciously," so both lessons can be seamlessly taught together or back to back. The behaviors that make up this skill specifically relate to verbal invitations and offers. However, you can broaden this lesson to include discussions about printed or written invitations, such as e-cards, e-texts and e-mails. Issues worth discussing include when a written or verbal invitation is more appropriate, style (formal versus informal), word choice, spelling and slang. These issues can lead to lively debates that encourage students to think critically about social relationships and etiquette.

Proactive Teaching Interaction

Introduce the Skill

Have students brainstorm reasons why it is important to know how to properly extend an offer or invitation. Reasons can include:

- Demonstrates good manners
- Shows respect
- Makes others feel special or appreciated
- Helps you get a "Yes" answer

Describe the Appropriate Behavior or Skill Steps

Extending an Offer or Invitation

1. Choose an appropriate time and place to extend the invitation.

- Be respectful toward those who are being invited, as well as those who are not.

  - If you're an older teen who is asking someone out on a first date, ask him or her privately in person; don't text message or pass a note in class.

  - If you're having a birthday party and can invite only a limited number of friends, don't ask the people you're going to invite in front of other friends or classmates.

2. Look at the person.

- You make the invitation more genuine and meaningful when you give the person your full attention.

3. Use a pleasant or happy voice tone.

- Avoid mumbling or sounding insincere; otherwise, the person may think you don't really want him or her to say "Yes."

4. Extend the invitation.

- Say something like, "I'm having a birthday party on Saturday night and would really like you to come" or "I'm inviting friends over for movie night this Friday. Can you come?"

- Provide more information if needed, such as time, place, transportation, etc.

5. Request a timely response.

- When you need a "Yes" or "No" answer by a specific time, say something like "Please let me know by…."

6. Politely end the conversation.

- Say something like, "Hope you can make it" or "I'll see you there."

Give a Reason or Rationale

Throughout your life, there will be countless instances where you will want to invite someone to be part of an event. Whether you want someone to join you for lunch, help you with a task, attend a party or go on a date, you can improve your odds of getting a "Yes" answer if your offer is polite and sincere. Other benefits of knowing how to extend an offer or invitation include:

- When you ask politely, you are more likely to get a courteous reply, even if it is a "No."

- When you take other people's feelings and needs into consideration, you are more likely to receive the same consideration from them.

- When you invite others to be part of your life, they are more likely to include you in theirs.

Suggested Activities

Language Arts: Have students write two short stories. In one, the main character follows the steps of the skill and ends up having a fun party attended by lots of friends. In the other, the main character doesn't follow the steps of the skill and is disappointed when very few people come to the party and there is little fun.

Social Studies: Have students find a newspaper or magazine article that describes a situation where the United States extended help or assistance to a country or region of the world that was dealing with a massive natural disaster. Discuss why some countries are more willing to accept offers of help from the United States and others are not.

Extending an Offer or Invitation
Suggested Role-Plays

Teacher Note:

Have students select one of the following scenarios to role-play in class.

1. You want to invite five friends to your house for a sleepover, but your parents will allow you to invite only two. Show how you would invite two of your five friends.

2. You want to invite Kelly to the school dance. Show or describe a proper invitation.

3. You are having a big birthday party next weekend and everyone in your class is welcome to attend. Show how you would extend an invitation to everyone in the class.

4. The school librarian needs volunteers to reorganize the bookshelves. Show how you would ask a friend to join you in helping out the librarian.

Extending an Offer
or Invitation
Think Sheet

Name_____ Date _____

List reasons why it can sometimes be hard to extend an offer or invitation properly, and then describe how you would overcome that problem.

-
-
-
-

What negative consequences or outcomes might you experience if you do not know how to extend an offer or invitation?

List reasons why it is important to know how to extend an offer or invitation:

- ■

- ■

- ■

- ■

How can the skill of **Extending an Offer or Invitation** help you at school?

How can the skill of **Extending an Offer or Invitation** help you outside of school?

Extending an Offer or Invitation

1. Choose an appropriate time and place to extend the invitation.

2. Look at the person.

3. Use a pleasant or happy voice tone.

4. Extend the invitation.

5. Request a timely response.

6. Politely end the conversation.

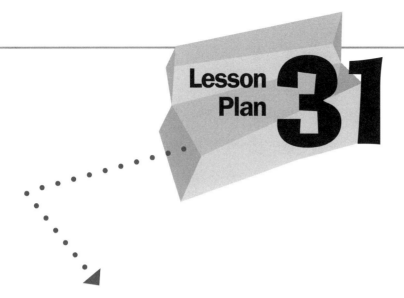

Declining an Offer or Invitation Graciously

Teacher Notes

Declining an offer or invitation can be a socially awkward moment for anyone, but it's especially treacherous for adolescents. Because they put such a high value on their social status and friendships, turning down an invitation (regardless if they want to accept but can't or they can accept but won't) is never simple or easy. If students handle these situations poorly, the resulting disappointment, embarrassment and bitterness can create tension and hostility in the classroom.

Proactive Teaching Interaction

Introduce the Skill

Ask students to describe situations where they had to turn down an offer or invitation. If any situation or experience turned out badly or led to hurt feelings, ask for suggestions on how the situation could have been dealt with better. Encourage students to discuss potential consequences or outcomes.

Have students brainstorm reasons why it is important to know how to decline an invitation or offer graciously. Reasons can include:

- Shows respect
- Maintains a positive relationship
- Demonstrates politeness
- Prevents hurt feelings

Describe the Appropriate Behavior or Skill Step

Declining an Offer or Invitation Graciously

1. **Look at the person.**
   - Eye contact communicates respect for the other person's feelings.

2. **Use a calm, pleasant voice tone.**
   - Don't sound condescending ("Get real!"), snotty ("Noooo waaaaay!") or angry ("Get lost!").

3. **Thank the person for the invitation or offer.**
   - Say something like, "Thank you for thinking of me."

4. **Give a reason why you cannot or do not wish to accept.**
   - Say something like, "I won't be able to because...."

5. **Offer an alternative activity or suggest another time.**
   - Say something like, "Maybe we should go to the park instead?" or "I can't go now, but maybe next week?"

Give a Reason or Rationale

Knowing how to decline an offer or invitation graciously is a skill you will use throughout your life. Most of you have been invited to birthday parties and sleepovers, or have been asked to go to the movies, join a team or go on a date. These invitations may conflict with other obligations, have little interest to you or be inappropriate. Regardless of the reason, saying "No" graciously helps you avoid hurting others and looking ungrateful. Other benefits of knowing how to decline an invitation or offer graciously include:

- You won't damage a friendship or relationship.

- You won't alienate yourself from others.

- If it was something you wanted to do, you may get asked again in the future.

- If it was something that was risky or inappropriate, you demonstrate maturity and a willingness to do what's right.

Suggested Activities

Language Arts: Have students think of situations where this skill would be used and then work in groups to write a one-act play with characters who possess and lack this skill. Ask students to create enough characters so every member of the group can be an actor in the play. After students perform their skits, have the audience identify the characters who used the skill successfully and those who did not. Ask students what lessons they learned from the skit.

Government/History: George Washington, after serving one term as president of the United States, hoped to return to private life. However, his popularity, combined with pressure from his colleagues, forced him to reluctantly agree to serve a second four-year term. While Washington's popularity would have ensured him a third term in office, he refused. On the board or overhead, write the following excerpt from Washington's farewell letter to the American public announcing his decision not to accept a third term. Read the excerpt aloud and ask students to judge how gracious or appropriate his comments were. Have them cite specific words or phrases from the excerpt to defend their answers. Lead a class discussion about how declining an offer graciously can reflect a person's character.

"The period for a new election of a citizen to administer the executive government of the United States being not far distant, and the time actually arrived when your thoughts must be employed in designating the person who is to be clothed with that important trust, it appears to me proper, especially as it may conduce to a more distinct expression of the public voice, that I should now apprise you of the resolution I have formed, to decline being considered among the number of those out of whom a choice is to be made."

Declining an Offer or Invitation Graciously
Suggested Role-Plays

Teacher Note:
Have students select one of the following scenarios to role-play in class.

1. Your friend invites you to see a movie, but it's one you have already seen. You don't want to go again. Following the steps of the skill, decline your friend's offer.

2. Someone you do not like asks you to the school dance. Politely decline the offer.

3. Your parents do not like one of your friends and forbid you to spend time at his home. However, he has invited you over to play video games. Show how you would decline the offer without hurting your friend's feelings.

4. A group of friends wants you to help them play a practical joke on your sister. You know she will get angry, and you'll probably get in trouble. Show or describe how you would decline to participate by suggesting other things to do that don't involve your sister or practical jokes.

Declining an Offer or Invitation Graciously
Think Sheet

Name_____ Date _____

List some reasons why you cannot or should not participate in the following activities:

- Go to the mall alone

- Go to a stranger's house

- Smoke a cigarette

- Pass on a rumor

- Join a fight

Describe possible consequences or negative outcomes if you did accept any of the offers listed above:

-

-

-

-

-

How can the skill of **Declining an Offer or Invitation Graciously** help you at school?

How can the skill of **Declining an Offer or Invitation Graciously** help you outside of school?

Declining an Offer or Invitation Graciously

1. Look at the person.

2. Use a calm, pleasant voice tone.

3. Thank the person for the invitation or offer.

4. Give a reason why you cannot or do not wish to accept.

5. Offer an alternative activity or suggest another time.

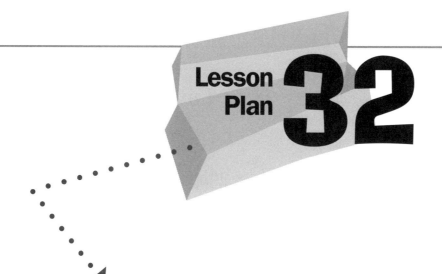

Resisting Negative Peer Pressure

Teacher Notes

Cheating on tests. Harassing students who are "different." Disobeying authority. Breaking rules. These are just a few of the unwanted behaviors students will engage in when they allow their personal insecurities, rejection fears and desire for social status to guide their decisions. To counteract the negative influences students feel from others, you must cultivate an environment where students value, encourage and reinforce positive and healthy attitudes and actions. By arming students with appropriate social skills, including how to stand up against negative peer pressure, you can improve the social dynamics and behavioral expectations that define your learning community.

Proactive Teaching Interaction

Introduce the Skill

Ask students to describe situations where they or their friends felt pressured to do something that made them uncomfortable or they felt was wrong. Discuss what, if any, consequences the students faced and ask for suggestions on how the negative peer pressure could have been dealt with better. You also can have students describe their experiences with positive peer pressure.

Have students brainstorm reasons why it is important to know how to resist negative peer pressure. Reasons can include:

■ Demonstrates self-confidence

■ Shows inner strength

■ Sets a good example for others

■ Prevents potentially dangerous or harmful situations

Describe the Appropriate Behavior or Skill Steps

Resisting Negative Peer Pressure

1. **Look at the person.**

   ▪ Looking at the person communicates that you are serious and mean what you say.

2. **Use a calm, assertive voice tone.**

   ▪ Don't mumble or act timid and fearful.

3. **State clearly that you do not want to engage in the inappropriate activity.**

4. **Suggest an alternative activity. Give a reason.**

   ▪ Reasons you can give for not doing something can include, "I don't want to sit in detention if we get caught" or "I'll be grounded forever if I try that" or "My parents will never let me come over again if we do this."

5. **If the person persists, continue to say "No."**

   ▪ Be assertive. Avoid going from a "No" answer to a "Maybe" and demonstrating behaviors (laughing, avoiding eye contact, etc.) that tell someone you're not serious or will change your mind if pressured enough.

6. **If the peer will not accept your "No" answer, ask him or her to leave or remove yourself from the situation.**

Give a Reason or Rationale

When someone persuades you to do something stupid (jumping off a balcony), hurtful (ignoring or socially isolating someone), mean-spirited (laughing at someone's misfortune) or illegal (stealing candy or using drugs), you not only hurt others, you hurt yourself. If you always give in to negative peer pressure, you never learn to stand up for yourself or others, and you make it easier for friends and peers to engage in dangerous or hurtful behaviors. By following the steps of this skill, you can keep yourself safe, develop a stronger sense of self and help others make better choices. Other benefits of resisting negative peer pressure include:

■ You will feel better about yourself and avoid feelings of regret.

■ You avoid consequences that may be difficult to live with.

■ By saying "No," you can prevent disruptions and distractions at school.

■ You can be a positive influence on others, giving them the confidence to also say "No."

■ You learn to cope with negative influences better, and it becomes easier to say "No."

Suggested Activities

Language Arts: Have students read Robert Cormier's *The Chocolate War* (grades 6-9), Gillian Cross's *Tightrope* (grades 7-10), Jerry Spinelli's *Wringer* (grades 4-8), S.E. Hinton's *The Outsiders* (grades 7-12) or any age-appropriate novel that describes how characters resist or succumb to negative peer pressure. Have students discuss or write about how the lessons learned by the characters in the novel can apply to their own lives.

Social Studies: Celebrate Black History Month, Native American Heritage Month and Hispanic Heritage Month by having students present biographical reports about the lives and accomplishments of prominent individuals from each ethnic group. Students should explain how the individual's life story embodies a particular social skill. For the skill of "Resisting Negative Peer Pressure," relevant examples include Rosa Parks, Chief Tecumseh and César Chávez.

Resisting Negative Peer Pressure
Suggested Role-Plays

Teacher Note:
Have students select one of the following scenarios to role-play in class.

1. Two of your friends plan to skip afternoon classes and go to the movies. They tell you to come along and not "wuss" out. Following the steps of the skill, show how you would resist their negative peer pressure.

2. Two students from your math class, who didn't do the homework assignment, tell you to give them your assignment sheet so they can copy your answers. Show how you would avoid giving in to their demand.

3. A group of neighborhood kids you are with starts laughing at and mocking a child, whom you do not know, because he walks with a severe limp. Show how you would stand up to your neighborhood pals to stop the teasing.

4. Junior is the class oddball who everyone makes fun of or ignores. There's an unspoken rule that anyone caught hanging out with Junior is a loser and is to be socially shunned, too. You don't like it when Junior gets left out, but you're afraid of what others will think if you try to include him or be nice to him. Describe how you would overcome your fears and what you would do to break this mean social "rule."

Resisting Negative Peer Pressure

Think Sheet

Name_____ Date _____

List examples of negative peer pressure:

-

-

-

-

What could you say or do that would help you deal with the situations of negative peer pressure you described above?

-

-

-

-

Why is it important to know how to resist negative peer pressure?

How can the skill of **Resisting Negative Peer Pressure** help you at school?

How can the skill of **Resisting Negative Peer Pressure** help you outside of school?

Resisting Negative Peer Pressure

1. **Look at the person.**

2. **Use a calm, assertive voice tone.**

3. **State clearly that you do not want to engage in the inappropriate activity.**

4. **Suggest an alternative activity. Give a reason.**

5. **If the person persists, continue to say "No."**

6. **If the peer will not accept your "No" answer, ask him or her to leave or remove yourself from the situation.**

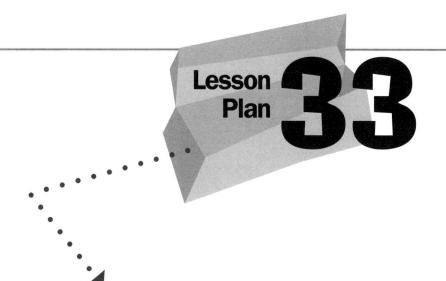

Responding to/ Reporting Inappropriate Talk or Touch

Teacher Notes

For this lesson, stress to students that they can use this skill if they are the victims of inappropriate talk and touch, or if they witness others being victimized by such behavior. Also, you may need to modify how you teach and describe the skill steps to reflect both situations (as victim and witness).

Proactive Teaching Interaction

Introduce the Skill

Do a "Golden Rule" activity to teach the differences between appropriate and inappropriate verbal and nonverbal communication. Draw a large T-chart, either on the board or an overhead, and write the phrase "How I **want** to be treated by others" at the top of the left column. Write the phrase "How I **don't want** to be treated by others" at the top of the right column.

Have students brainstorm specific words and behaviors (smile at me, say "Hi," be made fun of, get punched, etc.) that correspond to each heading, and write down their responses in the appropriate column. When both columns are full, lead a class discussion about their answers. Questions to ask students include:

■ According to the T-chart, what words and actions are okay and why?

■ When or where are students most likely to mistreat others?

■ How should you respond or what should you do when you or someone else is being mistreated?

You also can divide students into small groups and have them repeat the activity. When the groups are finished (allow about 10 minutes), have each group present its T-chart to the class.

Describe the Appropriate Behavior or Skill Steps

Responding to/Reporting Inappropriate Talk or Touch

1. **Stay calm.**

2. **Tell the other person to stop his or her behavior.**

   ▪ If you are a witness and are afraid to speak up because you may be put in danger, leave the situation immediately and find help from an adult.

3. **Leave the situation.**

4. **Find an adult as quickly as possible.**

   ▪ At school, seek out a trusted teacher, counselor, principal or other staff member you know.

   ▪ At home, seek out a parent or other relative.

   ▪ In the community, seek out a police officer, security guard or other trusted adult.

5. **Gain the adult's attention appropriately.**

   ▪ Say something like, "May I please speak to you privately?"

6. **Honestly describe everything you experienced or witnessed.**

   ▪ Report the names of everyone involved, including bystanders, and describe what was said and done.

   ▪ Don't exaggerate, cover for someone or leave out details.

7. **Answer all questions honestly.**

8. **Thank the adult for listening and taking action.**

Give a Reason or Rationale

At school, students who use sexually explicit language or engage in inappropriate touching threaten the physical safety and emotional security of everyone. Knowing how to respond to or report inappropriate talk and touch is empowering and one of the best ways to stop sexual and physical aggression from repeating itself. Other benefits of knowing how to respond to or report inappropriate talk and touch include:

- When you stand up for yourself or someone else, you feel empowered and realize that you can handle challenging situations.

- If you are a witness, you help keep others safe and reinforce the Golden Rule by setting the example you want others to follow if you are being victimized.

- If you are a victim, you can regain your confidence and make it less likely that you will be victimized in the same way again.

- You can help put an end to bullying and harassment.

- You improve the social climate and sense of security for everyone.

Suggested Activities

Science/Math: Explain what an IRB (Institutional Review Board) is and why scientists and others are often required to submit their research proposals to such a review. Ask students to explain how such a review can protect individuals involved in a research study.

Government/Social Studies: Have students do a research project on the FCC (Federal Communication Commissions) and its role in enforcing radio and television broadcasting standards, including its definition of indecent, obscene and profane programming.

History: Have students research the Tuskegee Syphilis Experiment, and then lead a class discussion about what happened, who was involved, who blew the whistle and how the whistleblower reported the abuse.

Responding to/Reporting Inappropriate Talk or Touch
Suggested Role-Plays

Teacher Note:
Have students select one of the following scenarios to role-play in class.

1. On your way to science class, you see a male student slap a female student on the butt while his friends nudge each other and laugh. Describe how you would report this incident or show how you would respond at that moment.

2. In the lunchroom, three girls are making fun of a boy who is sitting alone at a nearby table. Following the steps of the skill, show how you would respond to, and report, their mean behavior.

3. Standing at your locker, you overhear some boys making sexual comments about girls walking by in the hallway. When you leave your locker, one of the boys calls you a "ho." Show how you would respond to the comment and report the harassment.

Responding to/Reporting Inappropriate Talk or Touch
Think Sheet

Name _____ Date _____

What does the Golden Rule mean?

Why should you follow the Golden Rule? Why should you want others to follow the Golden Rule?

Why is it important to know how to respond to or report inappropriate words and actions?

Describe situations where it is very important to respond to and report inappropriate talk or touch?

How can the skill of **Responding to/Reporting Inappropriate Talk or Touch** help you at school?

How can the skill of **Responding to/Reporting Inappropriate Talk or Touch** help you outside of school?

Responding to/ Reporting Inappropriate Talk or Touch

1. Stay calm.

2. Tell the other person to stop his or her behavior.

3. Leave the situation.

4. Find an adult as quickly as possible.

5. Gain the adult's attention appropriately.

6. Honestly describe everything you experienced or witnessed.

7. Answer all questions honestly.

8. Thank the adult for listening and taking action.

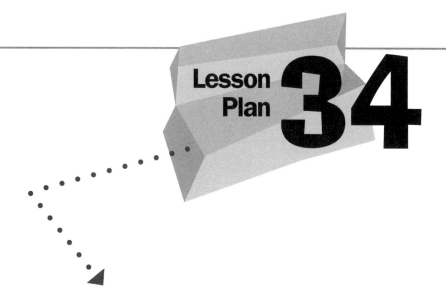

Reporting Other Youths' Behavior (Peer Reporting)

Teacher Notes

This skill is about keeping others safe. However, students often need help distinguishing between "peer reporting" and "tattling." This is especially true in the lower grades, where students are often told not to tattle but then are not taught when it is appropriate (bullying, fighting, self-harming behaviors, etc.) to tell an adult about someone else's inappropriate behavior.

Some students may not feel safe (physically or socially) telling an adult about certain peer behaviors. Therefore, it's imperative that your learning community provides a variety of reporting options that are safe for students, such as anonymous e-mail accounts, hotlines or drop boxes for notes.

Proactive Teaching Interaction

Introduce the Skill

To help students distinguish between situations where it is appropriate for them to come forward and when it is not, teach the "In/Out Rule." For elementary and middle school students, this rule can help them think about what they are witnessing and decide if telling an adult will help get someone out of trouble or get someone into trouble.

Here are the steps for explaining the In/Out Rule to students:

1. Think about what is happening.

2. Are you thinking about telling an adult to get someone "In" or "Out" of trouble? "In" trouble is tattling for no special reason other than to cause mischief. "Out" of trouble is wanting to keep someone from getting hurt.

3. If your answer is "In" trouble, don't tell.

4. If your answer is "Out" of trouble, then tell an adult right away.

Point out to students that when they help a peer get out of trouble, they make the school safer for everyone.

Describe the Appropriate Behavior or Skill Steps

Reporting Other Youths' Behavior (Peer Reporting)

1. Find the appropriate adult or authority figure.

- At school, seek out a teacher or staff member. At home, talk to a parent or other responsible adult.

2. Look at the person.

- Eye contact helps communicate the seriousness of what you are saying.

3. Use a clear, concerned voice tone.

4. State specifically the inappropriate behavior you are reporting.

- Don't exaggerate the situation; state just the facts.

5. Give a reason for the report that shows concern for your peer.

- Remember the In/Out Rule. You want to help your peer stay out of trouble.

6. Truthfully answer any questions that are asked of you.

- If you don't know the answer, say you don't know. Avoid making assumptions or accusations.

Give a Reason or Rationale

There may be times when you see a classmate, friend or peer engaging in activities that are potentially dangerous or harmful, but you're not sure how to stop it. In such situations, you should get help from a teacher, parent or other adult. Knowing how to tell an adult about a student's behavior can keep others safe and prevent problems from escalating out of control. Additional benefits of knowing how to report other youths' behaviors include:

■ You show that you care about the well-being and feelings of others.

■ If you witnessed something that was illegal or against school policy, you can avoid blame or accusations that you were "in on it."

■ It encourages others to act responsibly.

■ Adults will know it's a serious issue, and that you're not tattling just to get someone into trouble.

Suggested Activities

Language Arts: Have students read excerpts or chapters from *Harry Potter* (grades 5-12), *The Chronicles of Narnia* (grades 4-7) or other age-appropriate novels and discuss how characters dealt with issues related to keeping secrets or admitting the truth. Have students identify and explain any consequences characters experienced because they did or did not report the actions of others.

History/Government: Have students research the term "whistleblower" and find examples from government or business. Ask students to explain why whistleblowers are sometimes viewed as controversial figures, and if they believe laws to protect whistleblowers from retaliation make it easier for people to come forward.

Reporting Other Youths' Behavior (Peer Reporting)
Suggested Role-Plays

Teacher Note:

Have students select one of the following scenarios to role-play in class.

1. You find out that a classmate has an answer key to tomorrow's math test and plans to make copies to share with others. Following the steps of the skill, show how you would report the classmate's plan.

2. A group of students are spreading a nasty rumor about a classmate's home life. You know the rumor is hurting the family's reputation and that it is not true. Show how you would tell an adult about what is happening.

3. Your best friend has an eating disorder and purges in the school restroom every day after lunch. Show how you would help your friend by revealing the problem to a trusted adult.

4. A friend tells you that he wants to end his life, and he describes how he plans to do it. Your friend makes you swear not to tell anyone. Show how you would help your friend by telling an adult.

5. You see three older students push and punch a younger student in the hallway. This is not the first time you have seen this group of kids picking on that student. You want them to stop, but you are afraid to say anything, and there are no adults around. Describe how you could report their behavior without putting yourself at risk or making things worse for the victimized student.

Reporting Other Youths' Behavior (Peer Reporting)
Think Sheet

Name_____ Date _____

Is there any difference between "peer reporting" and "tattling"? If so, explain:

How can you tell when someone is being a "squealer" or "narc," and when someone is being a "peer reporter"?

Why is it important to know how to peer report?

List some times or situations where it is important or necessary to report other youths' behavior:

-
-
-
-

List some times or situations where it is wrong or not necessary to report other youths' behavior:

-
-
-
-

How can the skill of **Reporting Other Youths' Behavior (Peer Reporting)** help you at school?

Reporting Other Youths' Behavior
(Peer Reporting)

1. Find the appropriate adult or authority figure.

2. Look at the person.

3. Use a clear, concerned voice tone.

4. State specifically the inappropriate behavior you are reporting.

5. Give a reason for the report that shows concern for your peer.

6. Truthfully answer any questions that are asked of you.

Communicating Honestly

Teacher Notes

When students are not honest with you or their peers, misunderstandings, resentments and conflicts are just a few of many unpleasant consequences that can occur. While it may be impossible to prevent students from lying or shading the truth all the time, it's still important to stress and reinforce values such as truth and trustworthiness. In environments where trust and honesty are lacking, suspicion, doubt and disrespect flourish.

Proactive Teaching Interaction

Introduce the Skill

Ask students to define what communicating honestly means to them. Continue the discussion by having students describe the behaviors or words they focus on when deciding if someone is being truthful with them or trying to fudge the truth. Have students brainstorm reasons why it's important to communicate honestly. Reasons can include:

■ Helps you build an honest, trustworthy reputation

■ Builds character

■ Helps you avoid misunderstandings and conflicts

■ Shows maturity and respect

Describe the Appropriate Behavior or Skill Steps

Communicating Honestly

1. **Look at the person.**

    ▪ Make eye contact; otherwise, the person may think you're lying or trying to hide something.

2. **Use a clear voice. Avoid stammering or hesitating.**

    ▪ Speak with confidence.

3. **Respond to questions factually and completely.**

    ▪ Avoid speculating or making up answers to questions you don't know.

4. **Do not leave out details or important facts.**

5. **Truthfully take responsibility for any inappropriate behaviors you displayed.**

Give a Reason or Rationale

The foundation of any healthy relationship at school, home or work is trust. In order to have trust, you need to be honest. If you shade the truth or outright lie, you jeopardize your relationships and your reputation. When you're honest, especially when the truth may be difficult for others to hear or cause you trouble, you help bring closure to a situation and start the forgiveness process. Other benefits of communicating honestly include:

■ You don't have to keep lying to cover previous lies.

■ You develop an honest, trustworthy reputation.

■ An issue or problem can be quickly dealt with and corrected.

■ You don't suffer from a guilty conscience or regret.

■ You are more likely to be believed in the future if you have a history of being honest and truthful.

Suggested Activities

Language Arts: Have students research famous examples of plagiarism (reporter Jayson Blair at *The New York Times*, author and historian Stephen Ambrose, etc.), and then debate whether the writer (or plagiarist) was intentionally dishonest or simply made an error. Discuss how plagiarism can damage an individual's reputation as well as undermine the readers' trust in the media.

Science: Have students investigate cases of scientific fraud (Russian scientists' claims about "polywater," French physicist René Blondlot's "N-rays," etc.) and discuss what may have motivated the researchers to falsify, misrepresent or misinterpret their research.

History/Social Studies: Have students research a past political campaign (at the local, state or national level), and then lead a discussion about how issues of honesty and trustworthiness were used to "sell" a candidate or attack a candidate.

Communicating Honestly
Suggested Role-Plays

Teacher Note:
Have students select one of the following scenarios to role-play in class.

1. You took a friend's textbook without asking and lost it. Following the steps of the skill, show or describe how you would admit what you did.

2. While the teacher stepped out of the classroom, you and three classmates started playing around with the lab equipment and accidentally broke several glass beakers. When the teacher returned, she saw the shattered glass on the floor and asked you what happened. Show or describe how you would respond.

3. Your girlfriend asks your opinion about the new dress she's wearing. You know she saved for months to buy it, and it's too late to return it. You think the color is ugly and the fit is not flattering. What can you say that is honest, but won't hurt her feelings?

Communicating Honestly
Think Sheet

Name_____ Date _____

What does honesty mean to you?

How do you feel when you find out someone was not truthful with you?

What reasons or excuses have you used to explain or justify why you were not truthful or honest with someone?

Is it important to have an honest, trustworthy reputation? Explain your answer.

How can the skill of **Communicating Honestly** help you at school?

How can the skill of **Communicating Honestly** help you outside of school?

Communicating Honestly

1. Look at the person.

2. Use a clear voice. Avoid stammering or hesitating.

3. Respond to questions factually and completely.

4. Do not leave out details or important facts.

5. Truthfully take responsibility for any inappropriate behaviors you displayed.

Credits

Editing:	Stan Graeve, Terry L. Hyland and Barbara Lonnborg
Book Cover Design:	Anne Hughes
Book Layout Design:	Marie Ruhter